In Gardens

Udo Weilacher

In Gardens

Profiles of Contemporary
European Landscape Architecture

Photographs by Udo and Rita Weilacher

Birkhäuser – Publishers for Architecture
Basel · Berlin · Boston

Design and production:
Atelier Fischer, Berlin

Lithography:
LVD GmbH, Berlin

Printing:
Ruksaldruck, Berlin

Binding:
Helm, Berlin

Cover photograph:
Swiss Re Centre for Global Dialogue in Rüschlikon, Switzerland

Frontispiece:
Yellow stakes in a lake

Translation:
Michael Robinson, London

This book is also available in a German language edition
(ISBN-10: 3-7643-7084-X, ISBN-13: 978-3-7643-7084-8)

A CIP catalogue record for this book is available from the Library
of Congress, Washington D.C., USA

Bibliographic information published by Die Deutsche Bibliothek
Die Deutsche Bibliothek lists this publication in the Deutsche
Nationalbibliografie; detailed bibliographic data is available in the
Internet at <http://dnb.ddb.de>.

© 2005 Birkhäuser – Publishers for Architecture,
P.O.Box 133, CH-4010 Basel, Switzerland
Part of Springer Science + Business Media

Printed on acid-free paper produced from chlorine-free pulp. TCF ∞
Printed in Germany
ISBN-10: 3-7643-7078-5
ISBN-13: 978-3-7643-7078-7

9 8 7 6 5 4 3 2 1

www.birkhauser.ch

Contents

Reading in gardens

A garden rendezvous one Scottish November. It was raining, pouring horizontally; an icy wind whistled about our ears as we arrived at Edinburgh Airport on that November evening in 1999, with a sketch-map showing how to get to Portrack in the Scottish Lowlands in our pocket. The weather got nastier with every mile of the road we took that night through the bleak Pentland Hills towards Dumfries, and we became increasingly doubtful about the point of visiting a Scottish garden in winter. But as the year had passed the seductive power of the few pictures and reports we had seen about the Garden of Cosmic Speculation had got so strong that we felt we had to act immediately when a chance came to go there, even though it was November. We had been given permission to visit the garden, after a great deal of research and a number of telephone calls. "You won't meet the professor there, he's a busy man and likes living in seclusion on his country estate, but the Head Gardener, Alistair Clark, who has been responsible for the prosperity of the estate for decades will be pleased to show you round the garden," Charles Jencks's London office promised us. "You'd do best to stay overnight in the nearby Friars Carse Country House Hotel, and come to Portrack on Sunday morning." We arrived in Nithsdale later on that stormy night. We couldn't really form a proper impression of the landscape in the dark, but we finally found the little forest track that took us to the gates of the secluded but splendid former country seat, dating from the 13th century. When the heavy oak front gate shut behind us there was suddenly no sense of the stormy November night any more. Instead the enticingly comfortable atmosphere in Friars Carse came from the crackle of a blazing open fire in the entrance hall and the chattering of the guests, most of whom seem to be there for the fishing. We succumbed to the mood and made ourselves comfortable in the heavy leather furniture by the fire. The weather forecast for the next day was no better.

What a surprise! The Sunday morning was icy cold and windy, but welcomed us with a cloudless blue sky over the Nith valley. The low winter sun bathed the Arcadian landscape of woods and meadows in intense, warm light. We had scarcely arrived at the Victorian stately home at Portrack Gardens when the Lord of the Manor was cheerfully welcoming us and congratulating us on having wrested such a sunny day from the Scottish November. "Exceptional!" Charles Jencks felt he absolutely must take a few beautiful photographs of his garden in this extraordinary light, and so he said he would join us for part of our tour. Alistair Clark would then show us round for as long as we liked, "but please: do join us for lunch." What unfolded before our eyes in the next few hours and impinged even more profoundly on our consciousness through the stimulating conversation with our charming hosts over lunch was not just the outward appearance of an enthusiastically designed and lovingly tended garden. In fact what gradually emerged was a picture of a complex composition made up of architecture and landscape, science, art and garden, in other words a

Gesamtkunstwerk in which an individual world view had found its own creative language. "Reading" this garden, exploring its historically enriched motifs and opening up new and extended planes of meaning by fitting them together, made us begin to understand what stories this garden had to tell. This riveting experience is also available to people who do not like "gardens for intellectuals," as this is no dry academic garden: it does not use its linguistic elements, in other words its design motifs, randomly or without any consideration for concepts, but makes them into comprehensible, attractive and enticing places of immediate aesthetic charm.

In gardens that are conceived in such a rich and complex way, one is quick to set any site plans aside, as the planned visit becomes a spontaneous rendezvous almost of its own accord. A rendezvous that starts with the journey there, with exploring the surrounding area, looking for a way into the culture, the cultural landscape, of the country concerned. On occasions of this kind it becomes especially clear that the garden symbolizes the link between nature and culture. More than that, distinguished garden and landscape theorists like Bernard Lassus from France, John Dixon Hunt from the USA, Peter Latz from Germany, Dieter Kienast from Switzerland or Eric de Jong from Holland tell us that a garden is a compressed image of the world as we would like it to be. A garden represents our longing for paradise. A garden is a place of ecological insight. A garden is the last luxury of our times. A garden is a place of invention. And we are told that a garden is nothing if it does not seduce us.

Garden artists and landscape architects have always had to be skilful seducers to lure their clients, guests or other garden users under the spell of their lively, often expensive creations, which are unfortunately transient as well. Brilliant works of 17th century garden art like Vaux-le-Vicomte or Versailles would not have come into being if the garden artist André le Nôtre (1613–1700) had not had profound insights into the art of enticement. The garden historian Marie Luise Gothein pointed out appositely in 1926: "Le Nôtre knew from the outset how to introduce two major currents that dominated the spirits of these times into every aspect of his gardens, and to combine them with each other. One was the spirit of discipline, of fixed, clearly comprehensible rules, of proportion. [...] But this notion was also confronted with a tempestuous and ever-increasing desire for 'variété'. This society [...] would have been old before its time, would have died of boredom, had not an addiction to variety that is often amazing to us kept them constantly busy and excited." • About two hundred years later, Frederick Law Olmsted (1822–1903) showed an equal talent for enticement when he made Central Park, with its area of just under 342 hectares, into a highly recognizable green oasis in New York's strict urban grid. Faced with this massive task, Olmsted felt that the concept of "Landscape Gardening" that prevailed at the time would restrict the focus too much to the garden and the gardeners. He coined the phrase "Landscape Architecture" instead, and this caught on in Europe as well. Pioneering landscape architecture emerges today in the field of ten-

Gothein, Marie Luise: *Geschichte der Gartenkunst*. Second volume. Jena 1926; p.132

sion between nature and culture, between chaos and order, in gardens and parks as dynamic spatial structures. They are living spaces, living worlds, reflecting the world picture that predominates at the time, a contemporary feel for life. The very first garden, the Garden of Eden, was not just a place of successful seduction, it was also a cultivating intervention into nature's chaos, serving to create an ideal image of cosmic order. Our image of the cosmos, our world picture, has changed considerably in recent decades in particular, and so interpretations of the connections between nature and culture have become more diverse and more complex. This is reflected not least in the broad range of modes of expression in the fields of garden design and landscape architecture. Almost all the landscape architecture presented in this book, above all the private gardens, tell their own, often very personal story; they enrich the meaning of the places where they have come into being with individual traits and try to make people more sensitive to their built and natural environment. Not all the parks and gardens reveal their seductive intentions at a first glance and speak immediately to the senses. Some make an aloof stand, wanting to be approached patiently and to be laboriously decoded before they start to tell their story. And not all gardens are equally easy to read: each one speaks its own creative language, more or less imbued with familiar or modified motifs from the history of garden art.

The present's interest in garden culture and garden art was by no means taken for granted for a long time. There were times when such history was seen more as a chronicle of the constant human effort to intervene more or less violently in nature's eternal, immutable laws, with the utilitarian aim of directing natural change into regulated paths that were useful to man. After decades of imposing an ecological ideology in the seventies and eighties, and a one-sided emphasis on protecting and maintaining nature, for something over a decade now landscape architecture has been committing itself freely to its creative task – and at the same time taking a renewed interest in the history of garden art.

Cf. Burckhardt, Lucius: *"Gartenkunst wohin?"* in: Andritzky, Michael / Spitzer, Klaus (ed.): *Von oben, von selbst, für alle, von allen.* Hamburg 1986 (1981); p.256 ff.

The Swiss sociologist Lucius Burckhardt asked "Whither garden art?" in the eighties, and bemoaned the spread of unthinking, meaningless garden design that no longer seemed aware of its responsibility to make the world intelligible. • But now that creative freedom has been regained responsibility has increased considerably, and is faced with the deluge of images propagated by the media, there is one basic question that arises more urgently then ever: will landscape architecture contribute to the trivial background noise of interchangeable image worlds, in other words to a kind of Babylonian confusion in terms of design, or will it allow itself the supposed luxury of not just randomly filling the world with images and vocabulary, but enrich it with connections and contents, thus making sense. It is no coincidence that discussions about "less aesthetics, more ethics" • started up again a few years ago, and Dieter Kienast's earlier appeal against creative verbosity • still holds more than ever today, under worsening conditions in the competitive struggle between countless new garden and landscape images.

Motto for the 7th International Architecture Biennale in Venice 2000

Cf. Kienast, Dieter: *"Zwischen Poesie und Geschwätzigkeit"* in: Garten + Landschaft 1/1994; pp.13–17

The counter-reaction to exuberant, meaningless landscape design, as probably demanded at the current stage of development, must of course not end up as neo-traditional provinciality, nor in a joyless minimalism that says nothing at all. Providing enticement with a few carefully chosen resources, with expressive simplicity through skilful reduction to essentials, is one of the most difficult arts.

We find convincing examples from the past of rich, meaningful minimalism in landscape design in Japanese meditation gardens and the fascinating projects of American Land Art and Minimal Art in the late sixties, which many successful landscape architects chose to follow in the last decade. The impressive earth formations in the Mountain Garden in Graz, Austria, the Garden of Cosmic Speculation in Scotland, the Professional Training Centre garden in Holstebro, Denmark or the Jardí Botànic in Barcelona, Spain derive their expressive force from the intelligent placing of simple, artistically inspired landscape signs.

Many of those who found one-sided concentration on Minimalism too dogmatic in recent years are now committing to a much more lavish creative diversity that – as long as it is not accumulated trivially – can be equally fascinating. The individual, artistic garden worlds of Little Sparta in Scotland, of the Tarot Garden in Italy or the Rock Garden in India provide evidence of other qualities beyond Minimalism. However, the chief trait of these impressive artists' gardens is that they develop the compelling character of the world picture they are based on and the consistency of the story they tell in a way that is extraordinarily powerful and at the same time self-explanatory. The creative language of these gardens may show an almost overwhelming diversity. But the conceptual layers of meaning make them quite clearly and unambiguously intelligible. Anyhow, the trend towards returning to essentials has done landscape architecture good in recent years.

Landscape architecture has obviously also regained its interest in co-operating with related disciplines that work on shaping the environment, above all with architecture and fine art. The enormous complexity of current problems in environmental design makes unprejudiced co-operation with related disciplines urgently necessary. Hence today scarcely any competitions for urban development or landscape architecture projects are announced without requiring interdisciplinary co-operation. Fine art in particular has not just held its own in the past decade but has gained a firm foothold as an important meta-language for interdisciplinary communication. Mistaken approaches have been made only where either landscape architecture or art has failed to maintain an essential critical distance from the related discipline, sometimes naïvely or sometimes almost negligently, to the point of being intolerable. Landscape architects have sometimes insisted on "making art," and artists unscrupulously present themselves as the legitimate, indeed even as the better heirs of garden artists. The lack of respect inherent in such attitudes made it impossible for horizons to be widened and ultimately damaged the credibility of all concerned. •

Cf. Weilacher, Udo: *"Degeneriert die Kunst beim Gärtnern? Freiräume für Experimentelles"* in: Sprengel Museum Hannover (publ.): *KunstGartenKunst.* Exhibition catalogue. Hanover 2003 / Bianchi, Paolo: *"Künstlergärtner"* in: Kunstforum International 145/1999

The quality of the gardens, parks and squares presented here results to a large extent from good teamwork. The designs for squares in Lyon, France, the Varus Battle Museum Park in Bramsche-Kalkriese, Germany or the Swiss Re Centre for Global Dialogue in Rüschlikon, Switzerland are just a few examples of such fortunate co-operations between the disciplines. In many cases it no longer matters who was ultimately responsible for the overall character of the project or had the key idea for the winning competition design: ideally the different views and standpoints will have contributed to more open access to nature and landscape. Seeing town and countryside, building and garden, the artificial and the natural not as separate entities but as a coherent whole is often the key to a more profound understanding of the world around us. At the same time, this points the way forward to a complex and expressive design. Gardens, parks, squares and other open spaces conceived in this spirit usually permit layered readings and tell stories of charming complexity, a complexity that is appropriate to a society structured ever more diversely, because it lends a degree of aesthetic interpretation and abstraction to the complex reality that makes it possible for people to get their bearings.

If a garden is to symbolize the longing for paradise, it must be able to move people emotionally. Now that landscape architecture has freed itself from the fetters of planning on a purely rational basis and insists self-confidently on its creative role, it is allowed to arouse emotions again. And that is good, because the key point about people identifying with their environment is finding emotional access to it. Anyone who can build up positive emotional links with the built or natural environment is also more likely to take personal responsibility for the quality of that environment in case of doubt. Almost all the projects portrayed, for example the Osservatorio geologico near Locarno, Italy, the Hombroich Park near Neuss, the Park of Magic Waters in Bad Oeynhausen or even the Memorial Garden in Duisburg, all in Germany, create emotional access to different landscapes in a very individual way, thus making it possible to make the place in question one's own. These insights were neglected for too long in the marked faith in technology shown in recent decades. This lack of awareness was one of the reasons why purely functional, science-oriented green planning lost contact with its "clients." Who wants to know if the proportion of green space in the neighbourhood meets the quantities required by planning if these open spaces do not move us and or have any qualitative attraction?

Commitment to emotional quality goes hand in hand with a gradual acceptance of subjectivity. Emotionality and subjectivity may well not fit in with social processes that demand scientifically based value standards, pellucid criteria of evaluation, preferring to treat people like a predictable factor that has to be held in check. But it is precisely when designing our environment today that acknowledgement of one's own subjectivity – not arbitrariness – as a quality of its own is required, a subjectivity that is to be built into the design process in a deliberately responsible fashion. The secret of the fascination of many popular gardens, parks and squares, like the Jardins de l'Imaginaire in Terrasson, the Place de la Bourse in Lyon, both in France, or the garden of the Fondation Jeantet de Médicine in Geneva, Switzerland lies in the deliberately subjective approach to each place. This approach, sometimes seen as élitist by the general public opinion, presents a considerably higher risk of failure, especially in a knowledge society based on co-determination rather than a more objective design approach that is scientifically sound and backed by the agreement of the majority. But the greater personal risk of failure – common for fine art works – bears the potential of a work whose edges – metaphorically speaking – have not been smoothed off by majority decisions. Such works are not just intelligible to people, but address them substantially. An indicator of the quality of such "edgy" projects is often that public opinion finds them controversial, as emotionality and subjectivity never leave us cold.

Of course contemporary landscape architecture cannot aim to solely create gardens that are charged with emotions, barricaded refuges from a supposedly inexorable reality. While flight into the private seclusion of fenced garden paradises seems fathomable, public spaces scarcely admit such avoidance tactics. Everyday reality demands, not least because of the diverse claims users make on "their" space, a certain level of robustness and openness even to activities of a completely unforeseeable character. But public spaces like the Landscape Park Duisburg-Nord, Germany, the Place du Général-Leclerc in Tours, France or the Parc del Clot in Barcelona, Spain prove that it is not impossible to create robust public places that are open to a variety of uses, that touch the senses – and also tell us a little about paradise. Deep down we know that a permanently peaceful, paradise garden is a Utopia; Little Sparta in Stonypath, Scotland, the Black Garden in Nordhorn, Germany or even the Garden of Violence in Murten, Switzerland address this difficult theme astutely. And yet we occasionally enjoy withdrawing into an apparently private, superficially heavenly refuge so that we can dream the dream of a perfect world, at least for a little while. But nature does not "work" like that. Essentially it has only one lasting quality: the permanence of change. And change – as demonstrated not only by the sudden eruption of natural forces – does not always proceed harmoniously. So given that a garden cannot exist without nature – even if only taken in the metaphorical sense –, neither as an idealized copy of untouched nature nor as a cultivated manifestation of domesticated nature, then change is inevitably one of the most important system qualities immanent in a garden.

Whether horticultural interest has focused on the usefulness or rather on the beauty of nature: very little has changed basically in the biased growth- and safety-oriented approach to nature, especially domesticated garden nature, since man adopted a settled way of life. On the contrary, even the ecological and natural garden movement, which spread the radical motto "Let nature grow – nature will create its own order"• and demanded that gardens should change and develop according to the principles of ecological aesthetics, • but accepted nat-

Cf. Le Roy Louis G., *Natuur uitschakelen, natuur inschakelen,* 1973

Andritzky, Michael / Spitzer, Klaus (ed.): *Grün in der Stadt. Von oben, von selbst, für alle, von allen.* Hamburg 1986 (1981).

For a different view of ecological aesthetics see: Strelow, Heike (ed.): *Ecological Aesthetics. Art in Environmental Design: Theory and Practice.* Basel Berlin Boston 2004

ural change only within certain boundaries of tolerance, though these were set relatively wide. • It was thought essential at the time, on the basis of a physiocentric view of nature, that formal aesthetics should be completely abandoned in gardens in favour of ecology. • Nature was considered as the better designer, who would take care of aesthetic quality herself. Straight lines were seen as "godless" and "the right angle, once seen as legitimate and beautiful within the fixed structure of Renaissance aesthetics" was declared to be "a means of open space planning that was mindless, and thus inhuman." • Yet at the same time natural forces were forced as rapidly and effectively as possible to stay within their limits, if necessary using straight lines, right angles and a great deal of concrete. And how could it be otherwise, because of course this was not an act of avoiding "aesthetic catastrophes", but of keeping nature's life-threatening, inhuman and destructive forces for change in check.

Ernst Haeckel introduced the concept of "ecology" in the sense of "household theory" as early as 1866

Spitzer, Klaus: *"Ökologische Ästhetik – Ein Weg zu neuen Gestaltungsprinzipien?"* in: Andritzky, Michael/ Spitzer, Klaus (ed.): *Grün in der Stadt. Von oben, von selbst, für alle, von allen.* Hamburg 1986 (1981); p. 168

After conquering fundamentalist ecological dogmas in projects like the Oerliker Park and the MFO Park, but also in the front garden and inner courtyard of the Ernst Basler + Partner engineering practice in Zurich, all in Switzerland, a young generation of landscape architects is exploring a new balance between components of change and formally structuring stabilisation. Their background is not just a changed, more open understanding of nature, but also society's changing demands on public open spaces. Since the middle of the last century, and above all during the present radical change from an industrial to an information society, the general conditions of the world we live in have changed crucially; they are more open and more flexible, but also more insecure and unpredictable. Spatial structures of the future must be complete enough for use, but incomplete enough for subjective appropriation, and also complex enough for being able to respond to constant change. Newly emerging "untransformable gardens" will probably be increasingly rare and exceptional phenomena in these spatial structures.

While natural change is associated with growth and life and always seen as positive, decay and dying are also part of nature's fundamental processes of change, but continue to carry predominantly negative implications. In fine art, like Land Art, for example, but also in more recent artistic trends, there has long been a search for aesthetic strategies for exploring and exploiting the positive energies of decay. This has led to works of astonishing dynamism and openness. • Such innovative approaches to handling decay were not yet being seriously explored in landscape architecture because we have not yet really understood how to think and act in open processes. Even so, works like the Landscape Park Duisburg Nord and the projects mentioned in Zurich have examined how nature's forces of growth and change can be consciously included as active partners in an open creative process. This led to some insights that pointed the way ahead. In fact there has scarcely been another project in the last decade that so lastingly influenced landscape architecture's approach to metamorphic post-industrial landscapes as the one on the site of the disused ironworks in Meiderich near Duisburg. Growing attention has recently been paid to

Cf. projects by Lois and Franziska Weinberger, Olafur Eliasson, Fischli/Weiss, Roman Signer and others

components that are capable of change, first and foremost plants as the central, tried-and-tested medium of garden and landscape architecture. So finally some of the nonsensical barriers are falling that divide science from art, the "conservationists" from the "designers".

The everyday stream of prefabricated, seemingly immutable images of nature, landscape and garden that the public is constantly subjected to makes it considerably more difficult to create a new balance between what can and cannot be changed today. Therefore, knowledgeable handling of the art of enticement in garden and landscape architecture is more than ever in demand today: never before in the history of civilization have people been bombarded daily with such a variety of infinitely reproducible images of nature. In a society fixated on results and and alienated from processes, the predominantly synthetically created ideal images are embedding themselves very stubbornly, and feeding the urge for instant fulfilment. Questions about the quality and value of "authentic", changing nature are consequently threatened with complete oblivion. People's ability to perceive the different qualities of their environment is thus placed in acute danger.

But are gardens able to play the role of antidote to the wearout of nature images? "In the garden, we learn how to deal with nature without denying the creative forces within us. In this way the garden becomes a model and test case for the way we handle our entire natural and built environment," Dieter Kienast wrote appositely in 1994, • underlining the central importance of contemporary garden design, of current landscape architecture.

Kienast, Dieter: „Zwischen Poesie und Geschwätzigkeit" in: Garten + Landschaft 1/1994; pp.13–17

When we left Nithsdale the next morning it was raining again, pouring horizontally. The icy wind was whistling around our ears again, but the austere, wintry landscape that unwound past us from Dumfriesshire to Edinburgh seemed strangely changed. It was as though the garden rendezvous in the Scottish November had taken us out of the mainstream of our perceptual habits – not just for a while. Today, years later, we know that this and many subsequent garden readings have meant constant adjustments to the way we look at things. Reading a book can never replace reading in gardens, but perhaps it might entice us into questioning our customary viewpoints for a moment. It is almost impossible to expect more, but we would not be content with less in the long run.

In Gardens

A cosmogenic park landscape

Designers:
Charles Jencks
and Maggie Keswick
Private garden
Size: approx.
120 hectares
Under development
since about 1988

Can a garden capture the imagination and at the same time reveal the dynamic nature of the expanding universe? Charles Jencks, a distinguished architectural theorist and declared postmodernist is convinced of the fact: "There are many different takes on this plot, equally worthy of architectural representation, and they concern the shift from the view of a static cosmos to a creative cosmogenesis. Characteristically, architecture represents this unfolding in two ways: by signifying aspects of the changing and growing world directly (its laws, seasons and qualities) and by reflecting them abstractly, in new languages of architecture (or inventive moves in an old language)." •

Jencks, Charles:
*The Architecture of
the Jumping Universe.*
A polemic. How complexity science is
changing architecture
and culture. London
New York 1995; p. 22

Behind the concept of cosmogenesis is Jencks's view that the universe, contrary to the traditional models provided by religion and science, is not a precise mechanism, but a process whose history is shaped by creative, surprising organizational leaps. In his 1995 book *The Architecture of the Jumping Universe* the American architect explains his fascinating theories, which he has taught at distinguished schools of architecture in Britain and the USA.

In the rough, hilly landscape of Dumfriesshire in southern Scotland, Charles Jencks has been creating an extraordinary private park for about ten years now, in which the insights gained from his academic analysis of complexity theories take shape in earth formations, sculptures and garden motifs. Until her death in 1995, Jencks's wife Maggie Keswick, a renowned expert on the history of Chinese garden art and geomancy, was not only fundamentally involved in redesigning the 120 hectare family estate, but developed new forms and metaphors for the history of the cosmos, working with her husband, and supported by academics and

Sheep graze on the hills of the Scottish Lowlands around Charles Jencks's carefully tended Garden of Cosmic Speculation.

artists. This produced a strange combination of Chinese design elements and motifs from chaos theory and cosmology. The Symmetry Break Terrace, a lavish terrace in the terrain in front of the house, is a visual metaphor for the important organizational leaps the universe made as it emerged: from energy to material, to life and finally to consciousness. In terms of horticultural history, the terrace is part of the Earth Dragon of Chinese tradition, and also reinterprets the classical ha-ha, a step in the terrain that is invisible to visitors, used in traditional English landscape gardens to give the impression that the garden blends seamlessly into the landscape of wood and meadow. In Jencks's garden two retaining walls in natural stone undulate into each other to form this sophisticated boundary element. Its continuation, and thus the metaphor for the last organizational leap to the stage of consciousness, is in the form of a trimmed yew hedge enclosing the house on the rise in a wide sweep. If you follow the path down

from the house to the wide valley of the River Nith, you reach the walled Physic Garden, near a large greenhouse.

Jencks dedicates this kitchen garden, which Maggie Keswick designed functionally in the traditional way, to human DNA and the six senses – six, not five, as he adds intuition as man's sixth sense, and enriches the garden with sculptures and coded sayings. Four large aluminium sculptures symbolize the DNA double helix and represent the sense of taste, hearing, touch and intuition, as mentioned. The senses of sight and smell are represented figuratively as a larger-than-life nose and a cave with optical installations. The plants in the beds, which are framed by low box hedges, are such that stimulate the particular senses. So the sculpture for the sense of touch is surrounded by thistles, stinging nettles and stapelia, while the earth hollow that visitors can

The Symmetry Break Terrace, an ornamental terrace in the terrain in front of the house, separates the garden from the surrounding countryside.

In the kitchen garden, Charles Jencks's DNA Garden, theories about the human senses flourish alongside the plants.

The Soliton Wave Gates owe their extraordinary shape to the physical laws of wave transmission.

walk on around the nose is planted with aromatic plants like oregano, lavender and thyme. The DNA Garden is not so much intended for the cultivation of kitchen herbs as for an aesthetic approach to all-embracing knowledge, and it is not surprising to learn that Maggie Keswick was an occasional guest of Ian Hamilton Finlay in Little Sparta, which is only a few hours' drive away.

The creative and conceptual abundance of the DNA Garden is pleasingly balanced a few paces away by breathtakingly shaped mounds of earth and grandiose expanses of water. Their composition is reminiscent of the 18th-century, classical English landscape garden at Studley Royal. From the top of the Snail Mound, a grassy cone of earth about 15 metres high, you enjoy a wonderful view of the landscaped garden, fringed with trees and shrubs, and the surrounding Lowlands. The companion piece to the Snail Mound, climbed by two spiral paths that paradoxically slope downwards at times, is the Snake Mound. This S-shaped wave of earth about 120 metres long and made up of elegantly placed loops of earth encloses the three Slug Lakes, placed in the landscape like mirrors of the sky.

The garden's formal design language does borrow from elements of chaos theory, but it is questionable whether these are already the "new language" or the genuine "inventive moves in an old language" that Jencks talks about. The meticulously tended garden gives little free rein to nature's spontaneous growth and ageing process; on the contrary: the high degree of order in the design prevents natural chaos from actually making any unexpected jumps. But the garden does, on the basis of complexity theory, combine elements of classical English

The Jumping Bridge: Maggie Keswick, renowned expert in the history of Chinese garden art and geomancy, gave the garden its Chinese accents.

garden art with what seems like extra-terrestrial Land Art to make a hybrid landscape architecture that develops the language of garden design further and formally conveys a new and dynamic image of the world.

Snake Mound. The elegant formal language of nature and art in dialogue is reminiscent of the 18th century landscape garden at Studley Royal.

Impressive shadow play in the November
light around the Snail Mound, which is
reached via a spiralling path.

The background shows the
18th-century gatehouse, converted
into the study lab "Octagonia".

From the 15-metre-high Snail Mound, visitors enjoy the view of the Slug Lakes and the surrounding countryside.

The grandiose earth formations are based on chaos theory, but even for visitors without a particular interest in philosophies of science this is a fascinating landscape.

A garden as space for political experience

Designer:
Ian Hamilton Finlay
Private landscape garden
Size: approx. 1.5 hectares
Under development
since 1966

The story of a little park that now counts as one of the classic examples of modern garden design began 33 years ago in the bleak moorland near the Pentland Hills in the Scottish Lowlands. This *Gesamtkunstwerk* was not created by either a brilliant garden artist or a landscape architect. The poet and artist Ian Hamilton Finlay, born in 1925 and already internationally known as an exponent of concrete poetry more than 40 years ago, moved into the abandoned and derelict farmhouse at Stonypath with his wife and child in 1966. He was almost penniless and completely inexperienced in garden design, but inspired by a vision. He transformed the wild estate, which covers over one and a half hectares, into a poet's garden, using the most primitive of means. Finlay's love of concrete poetry demanded more than a vegetable garden to provide for his young family. He started by placing artefacts in the garden. Anyone visiting Little Sparta today follows a bumpy path through the sheep fields and has to deal with three gates to arrive in a paradisal garden realm with a finely-tuned composition of trees, bushes, perennials and artworks.

Taking the early English landscape gardens created by poets, philosophers and politicians in the 18th century as a precise model, the selection and placing of the sculptures is not left to chance in Finlay's Little Sparta, but works to a philosophical programme that resists the total secularization of our culture. Exploring the intricately designed sections with resounding names like Roman Garden, Epicurean Garden or Julie's Garden is like a journey through the sagas of classical antiquity, enriched with relics from the whole of European cultural history. In the

This area in front of his house, protected against the wind by a hedge, is where Finlay tends his potted plants.

The Garden Temple by the pool, a converted barn, forms the spiritual centre of the garden.

Secluded garden paths, accompanied by sculptures in the form of filled fruit baskets, lead through Finlay's garden realm.

grove of trees you come across pyramids and fragments of columns, stones are engraved with sayings, busts of Epicurus and Hypnos create sacred spots and the formally mundane equipment shed has been transformed into a garden temple of Apollo.

As Finlay struggles with the superficiality of today's time, his garden has taken on neoclassical traits. His return to classical traditions and values is based on his conviction that man must take full responsibility for his actions at all times in the interests of further cultural development, and must not give up his will and bow to current trends towards political, ecological and social correctness. Finlay will take anything on if this conviction has to be defended. When his garden temple was threatened with taxation as a commercial building in 1983, he started a sensational struggle with the fiscal authorities. The "Monument to the First Battle of Little Sparta" is evidence of his unshakeable will to stand up to secular powers.

Classical garden elements harbour a range of historical allusions in the Woodland Garden, an idyllic grove of trees.

In his art, this controversial poet draws on the French Revolution in particular, which he sees as a perfect example of the dialectic between art and nature. His poems carved into stone, sayings and quotations create their own stratum of meaning in landscape and garden and trigger a wide range of associations and interpretations for the viewer. Thus for example he had a quotation from the French revolutionary Louis Antoine Saint-Just carved in individual stone blocks word by word: THE PRESENT ORDER IS THE DISORDER OF THE FUTURE. SAINT-JUST. Anyone who was in a position to switch the stones around could change the quotation and its meaning constantly. In the spirit of an open artwork this game gives viewers the opportunity to change the viewpoint, experience new meanings, and understand "revolution". Conventional standpoints in contemporary thought suddenly start to seem less stable.

But Finlay thinks nothing of intellectual indoctrination and does not force visitors to come to terms with his work. If anyone seeks advice, however, he patiently explains what this or that apparently myster-

The Nuclear Sail thrusts up out of the Arcadian pastures of the Scottish Lowlands, a reminder of threats lurking below the visible surface.

Lochan Eck, a little reservoir, is wonderfully embedded in the rough moorland.

ious inscription in the garden is all about. But the poet, who leads a very secluded life, is just as pleased if visitors are enthused by the lovingly tended garden landscape and the fragrant glory of the flowers.

The warlike symbolism we are confronted with in Finlay's garden realm disturbs many unprepared visitors and is not uncontroversial. It is a sharp and witty comment on the contemporary interpretation of Arcadia: a small sculpture of an aircraft carrier, a kind of topical translation of the Roman galleys in the gardens of the Villa d'Este in Tivoli, reminds us of our world's war theatres and functions as a bird feeder. The Tank Leader crawls out of the flowerbed yet it is only a harmless bronze tortoise, which of course has its armour with it. Finlay reminds us that the seemingly Arcadian culture landscape is a result of the eternal conflict between man and nature, of man's constant war with his own kind.

Finlay does not want to make this violent component of cultural development, which is necessary in his eyes, taboo. He is aiming at the problem zones of a society that would like to suppress and forget anything violent. Understandably, this kind of open criticism is often rejected because it threatens to shatter the bourgeois world picture, and so Finlay has a lot to tell about disputes from which he did not always emerge victorious.

Finlay's garden, like all his work as an artist, has found vehement critics and enthusiastic admirers all over the world. Little Sparta is neither a fashionable sculpture park nor a naïve or frivolous hermitage. Here a piece of landscape has been cultivated as a garden, and at the same time, minimal poetic and sculptural interventions have turned it into a sensual and significant place that influences viewers' cultural perceptions. The garden is based on a precise concept in terms of its meaning, and in this it is different from many current garden and landscape designs that are based only on functional thinking or formal loquacity.

The little tablet with the inscription AD in the mountain ashes alludes to Albrecht Dürer's nature studies.

Simple, mown paths over the fields lead from the garden into the surrounding area, accompanied by accessible sculptures like the Hegel Stile.

The eye is drawn into the sweep of the landscape as if through a window by the magnificent blossom in the intimate Sunken Garden.

Little Sparta in Stonypath   33

Symbolic readings

Landscape architect:
Torben Schønherr
Garden for a
communal facility
Size: approx.
3 hectares
Completed in 1993

Danish and Swedish garden architects like Gundmund Nyeland Brandt and Carl Theodor Sørensen were always a little reserved about fashionable innovations from nearby foreign countries. In the first half of the 20th century they developed a simple yet powerful and elegant formal language for gardens and landscape that – rather like Danish design – is considered timelessly modern. Nature played an important part in the great northern garden architects' creations. It had been necessary from time immemorial to use freely growing or severely trimmed hedges and groups of trees as protection against the strong Atlantic winds that swept over the gently rolling terrain of Jutland and the Danish islands. The familiar streamlined figures emerged, as if the wind had completely worn down the corners and edges in the Danes' garden plans, which they like to make geometrical. Where the sea wind can attack unchecked, it still models the silhouettes of groups of trees, making them into striking, sometimes bizarre shapes that populate the landscape and men's imaginations like restless spirits.

A fragment of a whitebeam hedge that had been shaped by the wind in this way also remained in the park-like garden of the AMU professional training centre in Holstebro. It still tells us something about the history of the landscape, even though the site has been part of an extensive industrial estate for a long time, and is now sheltered from the nearby ring road and the open countryside by a noise barrier. In 1994, the Danish landscape architect and poet Torben Schønherr was commissioned to plant the large noise barrier and create a low-maintenance garden between the low wings of the new training centre.

Landscape, architecture and art combine to form a simple ensemble.

The landscape architect dealt with planting the noise barrier in a typically Danish way by laying a thick mat of broad-leaved shrubs trimmed precisely to knee height over the gently moulded mound, with their organically trimmed edges impinging on the garden itself from the outside. But this did not fulfil the actual commission of creating a meaningful place, as Schønherr aims for a combination of poetry and garden in all his projects. "For me poems and gardens are made of the same material – from nothing into nothing – and I like this combination very much."

For outsiders it seems something of a cliché that the Dane, when looking for poetic landscape elements, came across a motif that plays a central role not just in Hans Christian Andersen's fairy tale, but also in the romantic Danish national play Elverhøj, written in 1828 by Johan Ludvig Heiberg: the elf hill, the legendary seat of the elf king and his retinue. The story has it that on special nights the hill rises into the air on columns of fire, allowing mortals an enticing but sometimes fatal glimpse of the elven realm, for anyone who enters it will never return. And in fact mounds of earth several metres high do feature in the Danish cultural landscape.

In Holstebro, Torben Schønherr has created a five-metre-high mound of earth, 30 metres in diameter, constructed with geometrical precision. He covered the archetypal formation with grass, and divided the earth sculpture up with a knife-sharp, slightly inclined incision. He clad the cut surfaces with polished, reddish granite slabs that create a striking accent in the landscape of green grass. The ground plan of the second half of the earth mound is marked by a shallow stretch of water fed from a small, severely framed spring via a short channel. A rusty sculpture in Corten steel, several metres high, by the sculptor Erik Heide stands in the water in front of the reddish wall of the cut hill. This shape towers up in front of viewers like a guard, apparently forbidding them to enter the realm of the elves. Inspired by this image, people also think they can make out human forms in the gnarled, wind-worn whitebeams, obeying the watcher's command.

The design for this site in the middle of the otherwise utterly functional industrial estate is called "The Universal Second." With it, Schønherr is trying to express something about the origins of the earth and the fact that time was standing still at that moment, in a formally powerful and yet almost playfully simple way. Erik Heide's sculpture, as described in an accompanying essay, symbolizes man, as only man is in a position to formulate the concept of universality.

The wind-lashed whitebeam hedge, left over from the many wind-protection hedges in the Danish cultural landscape, inclines towards the earth dome.

But the archaic formal language the designer used in the garden, the untamed force of old legends and the irresistible attraction of Hans Christian Andersen's fairy tales tempts viewers to offer quite different readings, and it is almost like the forbidden glimpse of the glowing mound of earth at night: woe betide anyone who gets lost here!

The mound of earth with a cut in it thrusts up five metres from its flat surroundings and shows a narrow water-channel the way towards the entrance of the building.

The water in the park of the AMU professional training centre in Holstebro is like a mirror to the heavens.

"Elverhøj," the elf hill, is watched over by its severe guard.

Forest park with computer interface

Landscape architects:
West 8
Private park
Size: approx.
2 hectares
Completed in
1997–1998

The Dutch landscape was invented by its inhabitants. For centuries they have fought defiantly and systematically to wrest usable land from the natural violence of the sea. Rational and technological treatment of nature and landscape also characterizes Dutch landscape architecture, one of whose most distinguished exponents since the early nineties has been the Rotterdam practice West 8. The eminent head and founder of West 8, named after the prevailing wind in Rotterdam, and its force, is the landscape architect Adriaan Geuze, who was born in 1960. He has long seen the boundaries between the disciplines that shape the environment as irrelevant. He and his team of landscape architects, architects, town planners, designers and botanists take responsibility for a large number of projects whose hallmark is a delight in experiment, combining a radical approach to artistic landscape architecture with ecological sensitivity and creating a considerable stir internationally.

In 1998, West 8 created a town garden of about two hectares for the headquarters of Interpolis Insurance in Tilburg, a high-rise office building by the Dutch architecture practice Abe Bonnema. The triangular open space extends between the 170-metre-long insurance building on the north side, the new Tivoli multi-storey car park and the Popcluster music centre to the east, and a residential development on the southwest side. Holly hedges and a steel fence painted dark green form a border with the streets in the surrounding area. Nature and artificiality in a playfully formal dialogue: some of the bars of the fence are decorated with steel ilex leaves, some of the jagged leaf shapes were punched out of the steel plates.

Abe Bonnema's new building is a conspicuous landmark of the Interpolis insurance building in Tilburg.

The central entrance to the park is under the section of the building that is raised like a bridge and contains the monumental entrance to the offices. A timber-covered bridge, developed architecturally, links the shady forecourt with the sunny town garden. It crosses a large plateau adjacent to the office building. The plateau is clad in a heavy armour of quarry-rough Norwegian slate slabs, reminiscent of a dried-up river bed. According to the architects' plans, a pool of water was intended to reflect the building with its two towers over 80 metres high at this point, thus enhancing it even further visually. Instead of this, West 8 placed a counterweight to the heavyweight architecture in the form of a bleak landscape of rock slabs, structured by linear cut edges. A light grove of magnolias, particularly when flowering in spring, lightens the black slate plateau.

This surreal environment, full of contrasts, is complemented by a controlled swarm of verdigris-coloured racks; this is a public art project by the Dutch artist Niek Kemps, called "A lighter side of gravity, part II;" it was placed here at the client's insistence. The swarm cuts across the bridge's direction and underlines the connection between the forecourt and the park. The impression is that painted sheets of glass have

been put down here for the time being on drying or transport stands. In fact, the copper racks are supporting large panes of greenish glass, printed with semi-transparent images of workshops, workrooms and storerooms. Perhaps a first indication that this park is not devoted solely to the delights of leisure?

At the end of the bridge, you step onto the soft floor covering of reddish-brown bark mulch. The landscape architects conceived the paths and lawns in the architecturally splintered layout by borrowing from the ground plan of the office building. The open space develops along tectonic-looking faults that follow concreted ground plan lines. Sometimes the concrete strips become dark grey retaining walls, or walls that can be sat on, forming a three-dimensional structure. Wooden frames have been built into the walls, offering an invitation to linger. You will search in vain for a faithful, comfortable park bench among the sophisticated design of this complex.

Narrow water-tables, between 20 and 85 metres long, provide striking accents, giving the designed open space an unambiguous direction and thus underlining the strong perspective effects in the park. The pools too are slate-grey concrete tubs, their cross-section widening towards the top and forming wide edges for the pools. Wind sweeps over the raised water surfaces, ruffling the mirror effect and rocking the delicate water-lily blossoms. Water tables were a popular garden motif as early as the Italian

Long, dark pools of water, green lawns, black slate slabs and red brick chippings characterize the abstract view of the park from above.

Magnolias set lighter accents amid the debris of quarry-raw slate slabs.

Verdigris-coloured racks cross the slate landscape, public art by Niek Kemps.

The park as a landscape for work and play, particularly attractive to children in summer.

Elegantly cut water-tables, lying in the park like great mirrors.

Renaissance garden. In Tilburg, says the explanatory text, pools of water are the central theme of the garden, as a habitat for water-lilies and frogs. Actually, West 8's composition does not need pseudo-ecological justifications of this kind. Children playing exuberantly by the water, boules players concentrating on their sandy track and people relaxing with a picnic on the lawns think highly of this little park for quite different, more obvious reasons.

The loosely planted conifers are still too young to provide adequate shade or even, as intended, to stand up to the office complex as a green structural volume. The open plantation of Douglas firs seems a little bleak, and it needs imagination to see this place as the Nordic-looking wooded park it will become. But even today this park has an unmistakable, pictorial character. And it is not just intended as a recreation area: power and computer connections will, as soon as the

The park is able to enter into a dialogue with architecture only by setting powerful accents.

safety aspects have been settled, offer employees access to the Interpolis computer network, so that they can work in the park.

The way people behave, their environmental demands, their lifestyle and their self-perception have changed so much that the old model of the urban green space, especially the prestigious 19th-century bourgeois municipal park, has obviously had its day. Late 20th-century man, Adriaan Geuze acknowledges, is self-confident, mobile, exploits the potential of new technology and inventively takes possession of all sorts of open spaces. A new, opportunistic approach to nature is gradually crystallizing, and the urgent question arises of how easily almost any natural image can be swapped with any other in future as a background for human activity.

No flowers on board

The Israeli El-Al cargo plane with four people and about 115 tons of cargo on board stopped over to refuel in Amsterdam on flight LY 1862 from New York to Tel Aviv. Shortly after taking off from Schiphol airport the jumbo lost two engines one after the other and the pilot lost control because the landing flaps were damaged. It crashed at 18.35 hours southeast of Amsterdam into the 11-storey blocks of flats in Bijlmermeer, where 47 people were killed and many injured.

Following the precepts of modern town planning, the satellite town had been planned and realized in 1966 on the flat polder land as a "city of tomorrow," with large blocks of high-rise flats grouped around park-like green areas with hexagonal ground plans. But, contrary to the planners' intentions, Amsterdam's white middle classes chose to avoid the new, anonymous tower blocks and left Bijlmermeer's urban landscape above all to immigrants from Suriname and members of roughly 90 black population groups from former Dutch colonies. When the Boeing 747 slammed into the blocks like a bomb on 4 October 1992 it hit the very heart of a social problem zone that many people derogatorily called the "biggest ghetto in Western Europe."

By the barrier set up around the scene of the accident, a growing number of letters, poems, photographs, flowers, wreaths and cuddly toys soon provided evidence of mourning and consternation about the incomprehensible catastrophe. In particular "the tree that saw it all," a large poplar near the crash site, spontaneously became a meeting-place and memorial for the survivors. This silent green witness turned into the touching centre of a "growing monument" conceived by the Geneva architect Georges Descombes and Herman Hertzberger's Dutch architecture studio on the initiative of the city authorities in agreement with the affected parties in late 1992.

All those involved agreed at the beginning of this potentially tricky project that a traditional memorial was not what was wanted, something used only for an annual wreath-laying ceremony. On the contrary, the contemplative place was to meet the need for a certain peace, and for personal encounters. But at the same time, it was quite pragmatically intended to be a starting point for an improvement in living conditions in this problematical quarter.

The architects' overall plan calls for a district park that is intended to develop further. There are four main components at the centre of the growing memorial: the tree and the area immediately around it, the trace of the devastated building, the markings for the linking paths that were destroyed and a new promenade as the backbone of a green area open to a variety of uses. Anyone approaching the scene of the

Landscape architect:
Georges Descombes,
in association
with architect
Herman Hertzberger
Public parks
Size: approx.
1.2 hectares
Completed
in 1994–1998

Georges Descombes's "growing monument"
in Bijlmermeer southeast of Amsterdam:
a cargo plane crashed into the former
"city of tomorrow" here in 1992.

Individual concrete slabs mark the gaps the air disaster ripped out of the network of public footpaths.

Seats were planned along the main promenade, but in fact the residents prefer the wide expanses of lawn for their parties.

accident along this main path, which is accompanied by a row of trees, is moving along the route that the rescue vehicles and fire appliances used at the time. This path's strict linearity contrasts starkly with the character of the rest of the network of paths. It is accompanied by low walls with benches and tables built into them. These were intended to tempt people to spend time in the shade under the new trees, but it seems that the local people prefer to hold picnics and parties on the wide lawns, which are gently modelled in parts. Large concrete slabs are let into these lawns at certain points, marking the open ends of the network of paths that provided access to the flats before they were destroyed. The designers' intention was that careful mowing would make the pattern of paths stand out again between the concrete slabs.

Further along the path, a bridge crosses the deep footprint of the residential block that was destroyed. Georges Descombes and his partners decided to use a negative volume, a strictly contained channel with water in it, to symbolize the loss of the building volume. From the west, the footprint slopes slowly down like a ramp, leading down to the surface of the still water. Only now does one become aware that the surface of the water is gently ruffled by a rivulet on the side of concrete wall of the channel. A tiny spring provides water, and marks the point of impact inconspicuously.

But there is no doubt that the tree is the focal point for the site as a whole. Here countless flowers and souvenirs accumulate, as if around an altar. The surface of the square area around the poplar is covered with mosaics, created by the residents with little pieces of glass and ceramics. An architecturally designed, roofed wall element with metal grids and inscribed concrete elements takes over the function of the first temporary fence as a repository for letters or flowers. A structured white concrete wall curves like a wafting veil around the southern part of the little square, framing the space and making it possible to sit down in the growing monument.

Mute witness of the disaster:
"the tree that saw it all"
in the centre of the memorial.

A tiny spring on the edge of the former
floor plan of the building marks the point
where the Boeing 747 crashed.

The line of the deep ditch marks the ground plan of the block of flats in which 47 people died.

It was only shortly after the dedication of the Bijlmermeer monument on the sixth anniversary of the plane crash that the affected parties discovered that the crashed plane – contrary to years of assurance from those responsible – had not been carrying flowers, perfume and home electronics, but poisons and ammunition. For the survivors of the disaster, who have had to struggle with severe damage to their health ever since, "the tree that saw everything" will remain a special, unostentatiously designed place of bitter accusation in future as well.

Many of the people affected expressed their mourning by designing individual slabs for the memorial floor mosaic.

The "memorial wall" in steel, glass and concrete, created by Herman Hertzberger's architecture practice, is an austerely designed place for lamentation and accusation.

The concrete wall with relief frames the space around "the tree that saw it all" like a wafting veil.

Traces in steel

Designers:
Gigon / Guyer architects
and Zulauf + Partner
landscape architects
Public park
Size: approx.
20 hectares
Completed
in 1998–2000

Archaeologists are very well aware of the value of soil as the earth's memory: the landscape registers every change with seismographic sensitivity and ripens into a cultural landscape with traces of history invisibly superimposed on each other. If we were skilled in reading landscape, we would see many of Central Europe's peaceful landscapes in a different light. It is not unusual that the surface of an apparently Arcadian forest and meadow landscape conceals a battlefield underneath: this is the case in the Osnabrück area near the little town of Bramsche-Kalkriese.

In 1987 the British lieutenant-colonel and amateur archaeologist Tony Clunn found something here that had been sought in vain for centuries: the site of the legendary Varus Battle, covering almost 30 square kilometres, in which three Roman legions were crushingly defeated by the Teutons led by the Cheruscan prince Arminius in the year 9 AD. This saw the end of the Romans' attempt to expand into northern Germany and the beginning of the dubious myth of the liberator of Germany, popularly known as Hermann.

The archaeological excavations are by no means complete, but are likely to last until 2020. Public interest in the Varus Battle demanded an archaeological museum and park in which visitors can gain a glimpse of history. The Zurich architects Gigon / Guyer and the landscape architects Zulauf + Partner from Baden in Switzerland won the 1998 competition for the project with a compelling, essentially abstract, but convincingly expressive design.

It all starts with the large-format, rust-red steel slabs cladding the museum building, which in the main view looks like a letter L lying on its side. The 26-metre-high viewing tower gives visitors a panorama

It is hard to believe that almost 2000 years ago a bloody massacre took place in this apparently harmless landscape of woods and meadows.

view over the treetops of the 20-hectare park, conceived by the land-scape architects as an extended clearing in the trees. Large-scale afforestation and drainage measures had changed the landscape here over the years. It used to be characterized by the densely wooded Kalkriese ridge to the south and the marshy moorland plan on the north side.

On their march back from a summer camp on the Weser the legions of Publius Quinctilius Varus and their entourage – 15,000 to 20,000 men, women and children – were forced to move west through a narrow natural bottleneck between the edge of the forest and the moor. In the dense woodland, dug in behind a two-metre-high protective turf wall, the Teutons lay in wait for the kilometre-long procession and attacked the otherwise militarily superior Romans on their unprotect-ed flank. As the unfavourable terrain made it impossible for the Romans either to flee or form up in battle order, they sustained terri-ble losses.

The former course of the Teutonic fortifying wall is now marked by iron poles 2.8 metres high. They are placed more densely in those sec-tions where archaeological excavations have already verified the line of defence. A temporary forest of shallow-rooted aspen, birches and willows is being planted according to historical conditions behind the meandering row of poles – so that the excavation horizons that have not yet been investigated are not damaged. Longer-living forest trees

Fine lines in the countryside mark fateful paths and boundaries.

Steel poles mark the course of the former Teutonic protective wall.

Three minimalistically designed pavilions – to be seen in the background – give new insights into this historical location.

Archaeologists digging for evidence of the legendary Varus Battle change the place and demand careful landscape design.

The 26-metre-high viewing tower in the new museum reveals the traces in the landscape that have been made visible.

Markings on the steel piling show how the terrain used to run: the landscape did not remain unchanged, even without human influence.

The Zurich architects Gigon / Guyer designed the new museum in Kalkriese and gave it an armoured exterior.

The two-metre-long, irregularly laid slabs evoke associations of fallen shields, pieces of armour or tombstones.

Lettered slabs with contemporary comments make the landscape directly intelligible.

Quotations from Roman historians in modern pixel script describe the dramatic events in 9 AD.

cannot be planted there again until the archaeological excavations have also been completed. Thus the gradual progress of the excavation activities can be seen clearly from the landscape image.

Narrow woodland paths illustrate the Teutonic routing system, while the route followed by the Romans north of the protecting wall is indicated by 685 large Corten steel slabs. The two- by-one-metre slabs are laid irregularly, and evoke associations of abandoned shields, pieces of armour or tombstones, and convey a powerful sense of broken strength. 35 slabs were given inscriptions and quotations from Roman historians, and can be read as inconspicuous picture captions at the place where it all happened.

Only at one point, the so-called Time Island – a 1.5-metre-deep incision into the terrain – did the landscape architects, working with expert advisors, attempt to reconstruct a piece of the sunken landscape from the year 9 AD, with protective wall, wood and moorland. This is intended to give the interested layman a better idea of how the landscape looked in the past. Framed by steel piling, the landscape reconstruction looks as though it is in a peepshow, and at the same time contrasts with the abstract interventions into the surrounding area, which leave more scope for the imagination.

The architects, working with the designers Ruedi Baur, Philippe Délis and Lars Müller, intended to give visitors scope for new perspectives and changed perceptions of landscape. For this they also built three minimalistically designed pavilions. These rust-red cubes, also clad in Corten steel, are placed in the landscape like scattered offshoots from the main building. The Pavilion of Seeing and the Pavilion of Hearing offer alienated visual and acoustic experiences that could also be found in other contexts, while the Pavilion of Understanding skilfully provides a bridge to modern events in terms of content. On one side of the pavilion you look through slits at the former battlefield, while on the opposite wall, pictures of current wars are shown on video screens. Not a few visitors suddenly realize in this pavilion that they are not at a memorial for ancient heroes, but at a place where thousands of people were killed just as cruelly as they are being slaughtered all over the world today, almost 2000 years after the Varus battle.

A new view of seeing and reading the landscape is conveyed in the Pavilion of Seeing.

Heroic death in the tulip field

Designer:
Jenny Holzer
Public park
Size: 3,400 m²
Completed
in 1992–1994

"I think that when people come into this garden, which is too dark and too black and too regular, and then read the texts on the benches – it will be impossible not to understand what it is about. That is what I hope, in any case." • Unequivocality of meaning is one of the thematic concerns of the work of the American artist Jenny Holzer. Since the early eighties she has been known for using electronic strip advertising to place very personal, socio-politically committed and harshly lit messages for debate in public city places. With this project realized in the early nineties in Nordhorn, a district town in Lower Saxony, on the German-Dutch border, she chose a garden as her medium for the first time. Holzer felt that electronics were too insensitive for the project's location. For this reason she took the risk, with expert advice from the American landscape artist Dee Johnson and the local municipal gardener, of designing a municipal park by the war memorial "Am Langemarckplatz," built there in 1929.

Holzer, Jenny quoted
from: Franzen,
Brigitte: "The Black
Garden: Der Garten
als Anti-Memorial"
in: Kunstforum
international, vol.
145/1999; p.89

As the "Nordhorn Monument," this memorial was originally erected for the "gloriously fallen heroes" in the wars of 1870/71 and 1914-18. At the centre of the slightly raised, simply designed round arrangement is a circular sandy limestone slab with the names of soldiers who were killed. On the centre of this was a cylindrical plinth with the sculpture of a naked, kneeling youth. "It is the fallen who support life," the inscription on the plinth still reads today. But the sculpture by

Hermann Scheuernstuhl, stylistically speaking a work of Neue Sachlichkeit, is missing. The National Socialists had it removed in 1933 because of its nakedness and allegedly negroid features. They made the square, which was renamed Langemarckplatz in 1938, their preferred heroic memorial in the town. The new name refers to the battle near Langemarck in Flanders, where the German army was reported to have suffered heavy losses in the First World War. According to a report by the Supreme Command of the German Army in November 1914, young war volunteers, prepared to fight and lay down their lives, stormed and took the enemy positions with the German national anthem

The 1929 cylindrical plinth, centre of the old Memorial in Nordhorn.

on their lips. This story, deliberately made into myth and used for propaganda purposes under the Third Reich, in truth contradicted historical facts and was later revealed by historians to have been deliberate false reporting for the purpose of glorifying the war.

The town restored the memorial in 1959. The missing sculpture was replaced by a supposedly neutral bowl of fire. 23 bronze plaques in memory of the Nordhorn Second World War dead were added by the long brick retaining wall above the lower section of the park; there was also a plaque in memory of victims of political and racial persecu-

tion. But discussions about the place's controversial history and the name of the square did not start in Nordhorn until 1986, and led to Jenny Holzer's commission to redesign the memorial in 1989.

A tiny decorative apple tree, planted in 1989, forms the centre of Jenny Holzer's anti-monument.

Directly adjacent to the old, raised round memorial she created a second circular garden in the lower part of the park, placed in the middle of the clearing between old park trees. This new garden is considerably larger than the memorial grounds and forms a kind of echo of the existing arrangement. The layout of the addition resembles a medieval monastery garden, but it is also deliberately reminiscent of a target. Concentric circular beds are separated from each other by circular paths, and divided into twelve parts by two paths running on a cross pattern towards the central round bed. The bed edgings in red Bentheim sandstone and the path surface in red brick chippings underline the provoca-

tive character of the garden, but they also correspond with the dark red brick walls and steps in the old memorial. Five simple sandstone benches, two in the old and three in the new area, are also shared design features, reminiscent at first sight of the 1929 originals.

Many memorial tablets for the fallen heroes of the World Wars and one tablet for the civilian victims of National Socialism.

But appearances are deceptive. New inscriptions in German and English provide drastic descriptions of the horrors of war and make it essentially impossible to use the benches: "It is the war zoo. It is a landmark. Pilots name it. Burned all over so only his teeth are good. He sits fused to the tank. Metal holds the blast heat and sun. The ocean washes the dead. They are face up face down in foam. Bodies roll from swells to the open in the marsh."

In stark contrast with the shocking effect of these texts, the small Arkansas Black decorative apple tree with its black fruit in the middle of the new garden seems an almost grotesque cliché, cynical – or is it ironic? The Black Garden makes it clear how difficult it is to create an anti-monument that would not make anyone enthusiastic about war. It is tricky to link a wide variety of levels of meaning and perform a balancing act between a comprehensible message and traditional symbolism; Jenny Holzer was aware of this as well: "I probably over-loaded the garden with symbols somewhat. But when I heard that black apples really existed I could not resist them. I thought that

The Black Garden makes a melancholy impression even in spring, when nature seems to be waking up in the park.

would make a logical centre. Almost everyone knows this passage of the Bible: it seems to deal with man's uncontrollable curiosity about doing the wrong thing. So I thought it was right to have the tree in the middle." •

This garden in the shade of the old park trees gets its name and its strangely melancholy atmosphere from the fact that the whole of the slightly sunken site is filled with plants with dark to black foliage and dark blossoms. Black Mondo grass, dark-leafed geranium and common bugle with dark purple leaves cover most of the beds. Copper berberis, copper beeches and copper plums with their dark pink blossoms frame the site and create accents at certain points. One of the impressive climaxes in the flowering calendar is the blooming of hundreds of black tulips on the outer edge of the target. The artist planted white

Holzer, Jenny quoted from: Franzen, Brigitte: "The Black Garden: Der Garten als Anti-Memorial" in: Kunstforum international, vol. 145/1999; p.89

Holzer, Jenny quoted from: Franzen, Brigitte: *"The Black Garden: Der Garten als Anti-Memorial"* in: Kunstforum international, vol. 145/ 1999; pp. 93/96

tulips only in a small bed in front of the memorial plaque for the victims of National Socialism. The planting is adapted and extended in consultation with Jenny Holzer year by year.

"It is like life," the artist explains. • "You have to take care of things all the time, and I think the nice thing about a garden is that you have to keep taking care of it or it's a disaster [...] The garden was a starting-point for me, a new way of acting somehow, [...] a place to learn and to experience." This is how the American describes her experience with a medium that is new for her, insofar as it is a living one. Residents in and visitors to Nordhorn also have to collect their experiences with this unusual new generation of anti-memorials. Some of them reject Holzer's disturbing portrayals of death in a public space. The effects of

her anti-memorial garden are felt with a particular keenness in Nordhorn because they occur in the immediate vicinity of, indeed confront, inscriptions honouring heroes of the kind familiar from many other memorials. Jenny Holzer originally intended to have the inscribed plinth from the monument to the First World War removed because its message was politically questionable. Instead of this, a plan was made to plant a weeping copper beech that was to enter into a dialogue with the little black apple tree and underline the sense of mourning. But the Nordhorn officials would not approve this alteration, and so the confrontational edge of Holzer's project was unintentionally sharpened.

Jenny Holzer's courageous project touches upon a problem zone in our growth-oriented society, in which dealing with the past is becoming

"I probably overloaded the garden with symbols somewhat. But when I heard that black apples really existed I could not resist them." (Jenny Holzer)

The apparently harmless park bench as a bone of contention: "Burned all over so only his teeth are good. He sits fused to the tank."

increasingly difficult. For a world that prefers to see itself as young, dynamic and attractive, death is often just a fault that has to be plausibly explained so that normality can be restored again as quickly as possible. The world only starts listening for a short moment when heroes die – their heroism being primarily measured against the daily media presence of so many other "sensational" news. But the Nordhorn town council also showed courage by deciding to use the name "Schwarzer Garten" officially in 1995.

Black growth: mondo grass with black tulip shoots in the Black Garden.

Reading along historic city lines

Girot, Christophe: *"About Landscape..."* in: Auböck, Maria/ Cejka, Andrea (ed.): *Open Spaces. The City. Perceptions in Contemporary Landscape Architecture.* Vienna 1996; p.36

"For me the garden is indeed one of the rare places left on earth where memory, emotions, life and dead mix unequivocally," wrote the Parisian landscape architect Christophe Girot in 1996. "It must always remain a place that changes both hearts and minds significantly." •
When work started on the first Invalidenhaus (army pensioners' hospital) outside the gates of Berlin in the mid-18th century and about 135 hectares of land was allocated to the Prussian war wounded for gardening, this was not done solely for reasons of self-sufficiency. The invalids laboriously transformed the infertile soil into a garden landscape, coming to terms with their terrible war experiences as they did so. Almost 100 years later, in 1843, part of the gardens was turned into the Invalidenpark on the orders of the minister of war. The aim here was to secure six hectares against the threat of being built over by the growing Friedrich-Wilhelm-Stadt, thus retaining a space where disabled soldiers could spend time in the open air. Peter Joseph Lenné, the 19th century's most important German garden architect, landscaped the park and made it part of his overall concept for "decorative and border tracts of land" for Berlin. At the centre of the complex, which was now accessible to the public, stood the monumental "War Pensioners' Column" with a Prussian eagle. This was erected in 1854, commissioned by the Prussian military authorities in memory of the dead of the 1848 revolution. The building of a hospital in the northern section and the Gnadenkirche in the southern part further encroached on the park area towards the end of the century. The place lapsed into complete insignificance after being devastated by the Second World War and when the ruined historical buildings had to make way for border posts when Berlin was divided into two.

The reunification of Germany offered the city an opportunity to give a new face to the site, which had been neglected and was in part used as a car park. An up-to-date urban park was to be created, acknowledging history and preserving the old tree stock and the historical wall foundations. The fact that the Federal Ministry of Transportation, Building and Housing was soon to reside in the adjacent former hospital reinforced the desire for a prestigious complex. Christophe Girot's design won the competition in 1992 because he did not propose any reconstruction, but skilfully linked an urban square with a landscaped park in a lucid design concept in two parts. "His proposal combines nature and the designed environment, prestigious qualities and playful elements to an equal extent." •

Gottfriedsen, Hendrik, CEO of GRÜN BERLIN GmbH (ed.) in an information brochure on the experts' report. Berlin 1992

The eye-catching feature of the complex as a whole is a granite wall that towers up from a rectangular pool 56 x 74 metres in area, as an accessible sculpture. Instead of following the former Prussian central axis of the Invalidenpark, Girot oriented the pool and the wall north-south. He was thus relating to a universal system of co-ordinates, but not excluding memories of the division between the East and the

Landscape architect: Atelier Phusis, Christophe Girot
Public park
Size: approx. 2.5 hectares
Completed in 1992–1997

The reflection in the large, flat pool makes the sculpture seem all the more impressive. In contrast with the horizontal quality of the adjacent new buildings by architect Max Dudler, the wall seems to acquire creative dynamism.

West. The quarry-rough granite surface on the one side and the smoothly polished surface on the other side of the wall are subtle references to the former division of different systems. The plan does not just reveal a veering away from the former military order, but also a striking geometrical interplay of paving and vegetation that is used to master the transition from the hard urban square on busy Invaliden-strasse to the quieter half of the park on the north side, with its old trees, rhododendrons and sunbathing lawn.

Actually the park grass begins in the middle of the granite paving in the square, as a "lawn joint" about 50 centimetres wide. As you get closer to the park it gradually widens into a band of lawn and finally to a whole area of grass. Or is it that the granite surface tapers increasingly to the north and disappears in the last row of slabs? Maidenhair trees and plain park benches, arranged in rows, complement the simple interplay of surfaces by adding a three-dimensional line system independent of the ground coverings. In contrast with the casual arrangement of the old trees, the regularly placed ginkgos will in future spread their unmistakable, shady roof of leaves over the square.

Something that is scarcely visible in the plan is particularly significant in reality: Girot's sensitive modelling of the terrain, which was originally almost flat. Five steps lead down from the pavement in Invalidenstrasse to the square, while the central expanse of water is raised roughly to street level. The square rises evenly towards the north, and then runs over into the park, which is at ground level. Ramps four metres wide, flanking the square, continue the rise of the granite surface and end at the northern edge of the park at a height of about 60 cm above it. Thus the park is demarcated from its surroundings by a protective frame.

One departure from the competition design is that the children's playground is not set inside the wood-like stand of trees. This children's paradise, intelligently and colourfully designed, is placed on the northern edge of the park and separated from it by a low concrete wall. But the children take no notice of this boundary and have long since taken over the whole park, paddling in the shallow pool or clambering on the "ski jump", their name for Girot's wall sculpture. The landscape architect prefers to call it "track to the future" and explains that the climb begins 20 metres in front of the actual wall, with a path dug into the ground. Girot revealed a strip of the historical foundations of the Gnadenkirche as a precise extension of the wall, thus opening up a window into the past that it is possible to walk on. The ramp-like "track to the future" leads directly from here to the highest point of the wall, 3.2 metres above the surface of the water. From here a rushing veil of water pours down the structured front of the wall and into the pool. Yet again we have a view of the dialectically designed Invalidenpark.

A "track to the future," starting with the historical foundations then leading into the beyond like a ski jump.

In the shade of the old trees in the park the city-dwellers enjoy being close to the smooth surface of the water, with the sculpture they can walk on rising out of it.

The water rushes over the front side of the wall and into the large pool, creating a relaxing carpet of sound.

Seen from the square-like part of the Invalidenpark, the grey of the granite connects with the grey of the slab pavement.

Groups of ginkgos in threes mark out
islands of shade where it is pleasant to
spend time in the striped pattern
of the open square area.

The wall also attracts attention when seen
from the quiet niches of the park.

Girot sensed from the earliest days of work on the project that after the park was opened on the Day of German Unity in 1997 his sculpture would become one of the many symbols of German reunification in Berlin. In fact the symbols of unification and politics that are all too often pressed into service in Berlin make it more difficult to confront Girot's wall object naturally, and it is perhaps, indeed, too emotionally overfreighted with its gesture of decline and fall. Visitors to Berlin are not always allowed to experience the pool with water in it, and there are places where parts of the project have been vandalized. But on some nights the sculpture in the pool becomes the shining centre of the park and drives out any thoughts of superficial symbolism. Then the veil of water rushing over the front side of the wall into the pool is effectively illuminated and the polished granite cladding reflects the city lights. A place that was forgotten and had become wasteland for a time has returned with its old name and a new face to the public life of a city of the future.

White memory on a green ground

The Israeli artist Dani Karavan's formal language is often compared with the artistic perceptions of the Renaissance. Gleaming white concrete sculptures, usually in the form of well-proportioned Platonic solids that are placed impressively in the context of town and countryside, have gained the sculptor, who was born in 1930, an international reputation.

But you look in vain for Karavan's artistic handwriting at Duisburg's river harbour. Here he has transformed the remains of banal office and warehouse buildings into a sculptural landscape of natural and architectural elements, into a Garden of Memories that at first glance completely contradicts conventional ideas of a park. "It is true that by and large the buildings are of no particular architectural value, but they are beautiful in a way and contain architectural elements like columns, walls, entrances, doors and steps that, when they are revealed and thus detached from their practical aspects, acquire new significance and emotionally charged, plastic and aesthetic values," explains the artist. •

Karavan, Dani in the explanatory report on his 1999 *"Garden of Memories"* project

Designer:
Dani Karavan
Public garden
Size: approx.
3 hectares
Completed in
1996 – 1999

During the structural crisis in the Ruhr basin in the nineteen eighties, Europe's largest river port also started to decline inexorably. A large number of businesses moved out of the Duisburg harbour area, and as everywhere else in the region the question arose of how this large site near the city centre should be used in future. As part of the Emscher Park International Building Exhibition, which ended in 1999, the former grain harbour and its infrastructure was to be turned in an 89 hectares multi-functional service park. A municipal park was planned as the green heart of this project. A master plan was drawn up, and granaries, mills, and warehouses that were considered worth keeping were extensively refurbished, under distinguished architects like Sir Norman Forster and Herzog & de Meuron. After this, the harbour area swiftly rose to become a desirable address for firms and private individuals and a popular location for art, culture and leisure.

Zvi Hecker's new Jewish Community Centre, a remarkable example of expressive religious architecture, provides a core and identity in Karavan's "Garten der Erinnerung." It is firmly anchored in the physical and metaphysical structure of the place. It almost seems as though Dani Karavan, given the tone set by the sculptural architecture in the form of an open book, gave up the idea of adding his classical concrete sculptures to the urban landscape. Beyond this, the sculptor was concerned to use his unusual strategy to build something new on the memory of something that had been, rooting his work in the particular place in terms of content and form.

The façades of unused industrial buildings in rows on the embankment in Duisburg's old river harbour.

Dialogue between architectural worlds 1:
Zvi Hecker's Jewish Community Centre on
the left and the remains of an anonymous
functional building, steeped in white.

Dialogue between architectural worlds 2:
the ruins of a staircase tower in the
background and remains of the historical
city wall in the foreground.

Dani Karavan placed simple, rectangular
planted fields in front of the skeleton of
former warehouse.

The undulating lawn can be made out behind the white-painted concrete frame construction.

Robinias, newly planted inside the hall structure.

The undulating lawn is also one of the new, alien elements in the Garden of Memories.

All the elements of the park – with the exception of the newly planted trees, which were distributed in an open pattern – follow this strategy and are oriented according to the ground plans of buildings that have been demolished, or respond to the fanned-out ground figure of the Jewish community centre. Karavan traced the outlines of previous buildings with bands of white concrete and low supporting walls. He then cut connecting paths into this system of lines, some of them paved with material from demolished buildings he found on site. Two isolated staircase towers have iron reinforcement rods that still seem to be stretching out to join up with the buildings they used to be attached to, now demolished. These towers he alienated almost to the limits of the grotesque by having them whitewashed and planting a pine tree on one of them – one is involuntarily reminded of the medieval Torre Guinigi in Lucca. Familiar images are superimposed in our minds. The fragments of a steel truss system, also painted white, tower up from the grass like filigree antennae, indicating the former dimensions of a hall, while on the harbour basin embankment the white-painted concrete frame structure of a warehouse hall with skylights remained standing – and was planted with robinias inside. In front of this are three fields of corn, a historical cross-reference. The surreal-looking ensemble of white architectural fragments on a green carpet is effectively illuminated at night, on the basis of a concept by Uwe Belzner and Stefan Hofmann.

The "antennae" in the park are in fact the remains of old warehouses, guarded by a second staircase tower.

Adding new architectural elements has created a puzzle picture made up of old and new, things thought to be valueless and things thought to have value.

68

Karavan complemented this bizarre scenery with three separate elements: an undulating lawn framed in white concrete, a stone garden as a dry habitat made up of large lumps of concrete with reinforcing iron "growing" on it, and a large industrial weigh-bridge, accentuating the centre of the park like a pedestal. Visitors to the park are drawn by this rusty industrial relic and enticed into standing on the weigh-bridge. "Generally, my work is created for people to use. My art cannot exist without people. My work is not there to be looked at but to be experienced," says Dani Karavan. • Here the history of the place is particularly clearly in evidence; the question the whole park is based on is insistently raised: the basic question about the right measure, the weighting, the evaluation of history and memory, injustice and justice.

Karavan, Dani quoted from: Weilacher, Udo: *Between Landscape Architecture and Land Art.* Basel Berlin Boston 1996, p. 78

Enjoying the artificial wave movement – best of all on a bike.

New life has come to the embankment in Duisburg's river harbour: a multi-functional service park has been created.

Climbers on "Monte Thyssino"

Landscape architects:
Latz + Partner
Public park
Size: approx.
230 hectares
Completed
in 1991–2002

The summit of "Monte Thyssino", a mountain that does not appear on any map, owes it name to the German steel magnate August Thyssen. When the industrialist, who was born in 1842 and built his first steelworks in the Ruhr basin at the age of 28, founded the Meiderich plant near Duisburg when industrialization was at its height in 1902, he was already one of the major figures in the district and the industry. The Meiderich factory produced 37 million tons of pig iron, latterly in five blast furnaces, before it was closed down. The factory gates were closed for over eight decades to anyone who did not earn a living from steel. August Thyssen, who died in 1926, would certainly never have thought that one day leisure climbers would name a 14-metre-high coal bunker wall with a summit cross after him, and that the site of his iron and steelworks would once become the largest landscape park in the Ruhr basin.

The worldwide structural change in heavy industry turned the Ruhr basin into a crisis region. In 1985, the Meiderich plant in Duisburg was closed down and about 8000 steelworkers were laid off. This left desperate working families behind, and 230 hectares of post-industrial, derelict landscape, whose image is now shaped by countless industrial ruins, huge machine halls, blast furnaces, cooling towers and other landmarks. In 1991, the "Landschaftspark Duisburg Nord" redevelopment project was placed on the project list for the Emscher Park International Building Exhibition, and a competition involving five international planning teams was set up.

The prize-winning "syntactical design" by the German landscape architects Latz + Partner is based on the idea of not obliterating the traces of industrial culture but reinterpreting them with carefully devised interventions. The breaks and scars in the maltreated landscape were not to be repaired, but crystallized out of the rubble as pieces of remembrance. The landscape architects did not draw up an overall design plan, but revealed one conceptual layer after another almost archaeologically, developing four different park concepts and then superimposing them on each other. The water park is made up of the tangle of canals and sewage and reservoir pools, while the rail park uses the old

The sinter bunker after the Meiderich plant was closed down: yawning empty concrete containers.

track systems. Roads, transport routes and bridges also represent a level in their own right as linking promenades, and so do the many cultivated fields and gardens. Specially designed connecting elements, ramps, steps, terraces or gardens join the four levels of the park visually, functionally, conceptually or symbolically.

Blast furnace 5, an 80-metre-high steel giant through whose innards you climb to the top provides a wonderful view of the park and the

Ruhr basin. In the shadow of the blast furnace is Cowper Square, named after the great blast stoves. The area has been planted with a grid of fruit trees, which environmental protectionists first saw as entirely inappropriate in terms of the industrial past. The Bunker Gardens in the ore bunkers of the former sintering plant are equally experimental and provocative. Special saws were used to open up access to the massive concrete chambers and a whole variety of gardens and children's play areas were created inside. You can also look down into the garden chambers from a long blue walkway.

It is not only tended, tamed nature that comes into its own in the park. A special kind of very rare vegetation that owes its existence to the extraordinary environmental conditions developed alongside attractive everyday nature all over the site. Exotic overseas plants travelled to Duisburg with aggregate materials, and found a new home here. Industrial nature rose to become the most important design element and called for some rethinking, and not just in terms of garden management. Peter Latz also questions our traditional perceptions of nature with the Piazza Metallica, which is made up of 49 steel slabs each weighing eight tons. The 2.2 by 2.2 metre elements were originally used as cladding for casting beds, and had to stand up to the erosive force of molten iron at a temperature of over 1,300 degrees. "This produced fluviatile systems that are very similar to glacial erosion, in other words natural formations created by the force of liquid elements. I find that considerably more interesting as a nature symbol than some stupid birch tree!" says Peter Latz.

The Landscape Park Duisburg Nord was awarded a special mention of the German Landscape Architecture Prize by the Federation of German Landscape Architects, and internationally the park has been for a long time one of the most important landscape architecture projects

The sinter bunkers today: lavishly planted garden cabinets, secret gardens?

Ten years ago and today:
Delicate elements of garden art move in
among the monumental industrial
architecture.

Sometimes reconstruction seems like a
new kind of destruction. What will remain?

72

Ornamental green is now flourishing, protected by heavily reinforced concrete walls, making them into garden walls.

Just under a decade later the results of the reconstruction can be seen: a living symbiosis of old and new.

The Emscher revitalized: part of a wide-ranging clean water system since the mid nineties.

Industrial landmarks presented as part of Jonathan Park's lighting design.

at the turn of the century and has been acclaimed all over the world. And rightly so, as at the end of the industrial age there are many places facing the task of tackling structural change in terms of environmental design without forcing out the industrial elements of landscape history. Exhibitions, concerts, theatrical performances and other cultural events fill the open-air stages with life against an impressive industrial backdrop, filling the former blower plant, the casting bay for blast furnace 2 or the impressive power control room, a kind of cathedral of labour. After nightfall the park, illuminated by the British light artist Jonathan Park, invites visitors for nocturnal exploration. A new cultural phenomenon, intelligently questioning traditional ideals about beautiful landscapes.

Art in an artificial Arcadia

It looks as though Hans Arp's biomorphic sculptures were the model for this bizarre landscape of box hedges. In reality, however, this landscape was originally trimmed to form precise geometrical shapes, and was part of the strictly geometrically articulated section of a garden that belonged to the de Weerth family, a clan of industrialists from Wuppertal. They built their country estate in the once marshy watermeadows of the river Erft, south-west of Düsseldorf, in the early nineteenth century. The striking axial views in the old park have long since disappeared. These conformed with the horticultural ideas that were valid at the time by extending far into the surroundings, signalling influence and open-mindedness. But the old park trees, including a number of exotics, have grown to an impressive size and surround the 1816 industrialist's villa, which became an island site once and for all when the a river was diverted around 1900.

If historic garden preservationists had taken over the historical Hombroich Park, the box would probably still be trimmed to geometrical shapes, emphasizing the cultivated nature of the former garden artwork and thus making the contrast with the surrounding, functional agricultural landscape clearer. But Bernhard Korte, who was commissioned to redesign the park and environs in the mid-eighties, resisted reconstructing the architectural garden style – completely in the spirit of the natural garden movement of the day, and in agreement with his client: "Dominating nature by cutting, hoeing, breaking and affecting aesthetic piety are no longer necessarily essential," felt the landscape designer, and decided to retain the "natural" forms of the overgrown box plants. •

Korte, Bernhard: "Museumspark Insel Hombroich" in: Garten + Landschaft, 1/1988; p.34

The influential real estate agent and art collector Karl-Heinrich Müller had dreamed, ever since the mid-seventies, of a private museum in the country, where he intended to show his extensive and valuable collection of art works away from the city. The sculptor Erwin Heerich, the painter Gotthard Graubner and the art dealer Sami Tarica advised Müller while he was building up his collection, and together they developed plans for new exhibition pavilions in which art was to be presented "parallel with nature," in accordance with the initiator's wishes.

But where is there any untouched nature in Europe? In 1982, the art patron acquired the site near Hombroich, about 20 hectares, but the intensively farmed agricultural land – landscape exploited in the most modern way – that made up the majority of the future park area obviously did not fit in with current ideals of natural, Arcadian landscape. Instead of this, Müller wanted a garden like an Impressionist picture by Claude Monet, and Bernhard Korte composed such a landscape, but "not as a result of some design frenzy," as he stressed, but close to nature, resulting "from the sphere of plants." •

Korte, Bernhard: "Museumspark Insel Hombroich" in: Garten + Landschaft, 1/1988; p.3

Unlike the historical park, the landscape designer did not feel that

Landscape architect: Bernhard Korte
Public park
Size: museum island approx. 20 hectares, missile station approx. 13 hectares
Under development since 1982

The tower, built in 1989 by Erwin Heerich, rises monolithically out of the meadow landscape.

reconstructing the former landscape of water meadows was either inappropriate to the time or a piece of "aesthetic piety." Studying old maps, archaeological evaluation of aerial photographs, pollen analyses from humus samples and on-site excavations provided basic information about a time when the Erft was making its mark on the river plain largely uninfluenced by human activity. An 1807 map served as the model for reconstructing the landscape. At that time pre-industrial mixed peasant structures shaped an apparently bucolic, diverse cultural landscape. As a consequence, the dead arms of the Erft were cleared again, the water level was raised to wet the area, and ponds and new islands were created. To present the landscape-aesthetic ideal perfectly, numerous 30- to 40-year-old pollarded willows, evidence of a traditional cultivation technique and early tree shapes that defined the landscape, known today mainly from historic landscape paintings, were planted alongside typical riverside trees like black poplars and alders.

Fortunately, the initiators of the art project did not decide to perfect the neo-Arcadian landscape with traditional early 19th-century peasant architecture as well; otherwise Hombroich could well have become known to people wanting to escape from cities as an illusionistic open-air museum for farmhouses or the cultural landscape, but not as a trend-setting art and landscape project. The industrialist's villa, the "Pink House," was retained and converted as an exhibition building for old master paintings, water-colours and drawings, and the artist Anatol Herzfeld set up his studio in a former barn. From 1982 to 1994 the Düsseldorf sculptor Erwin Heerich created eleven exhibition pavilions, "chapels in the landscape," as Karl-Heinrich Müller called them. They are reminiscent of Minimal Art objects, and have been embedded in the harmoniously designed landscape with great sensitivity.

In the spirit of the classical Modernist ideology, the sculptural buildings were placed in the "fluent"

A collection of sculptures has come into being in the immediate vicinity of Anatol Herzfeld's studio in the park, in this case a tree-trunk clad in lead.

supposedly original landscape like valuable artworks. An extensive, tangled network of paths provides access. The landscape protection authorities do not allow visitors to leave the paths, so they move along gravel paths or small woodland tracks through an artificial landscape of architecture and landscape design in order to look at a wide range of artistic and cultural objects and paintings from all kinds of periods and cultural circles, usually in pavilions that have no windows, but are top-lit. A particularly intensive dialogue between architecture and landscape, between inside and outside space, emerges in the so-called tower, a compact brick building on a square ground plan. Formally reminiscent of a minimalist sculpture by Sol LeWitt, it looms up suddenly in the middle of the path. You will not find any art in the white interior of the tower, but four tall, narrow windows, looking like paintings in the empty space at first, allow you to enjoy framed views of the park: the colours seem to become more intense, you hear the noises around you more clearly, feel your senses becoming more acute.

The Hombroich cultural area, known as the Stiftung Insel Hombroich since 1997, is a process, and so it is not just the naturally tended meadow vegetation that flourishes magnificently. The project itself develops ambitiously, linking cultural and scientific initiatives and conquering new space: in 1994, Karl-Heinrich Müller acquired the site of a disused NATO missile base. It covers about 13 hectares and is on a windy eminence not far from the museum park. The aim was to create a forward-looking "spaceplacelab": in future the site and surrounding terrain will become a new kind of experimental urban landscape, an ensemble of 14 so-called quarters, designed by Daniel Libeskind, Krischanitz Frank Architekten, Alvaro Siza, Frei Otto, Raimund Abraham,

A bridge fringed with hydrangeas in front of Erwin Heerich's High Gallery.

Fundamentally, the tower – like all Erwin Heerich's other buildings in the park – is an architectural sculpture tending to the minimal.

The Parliament, another steel sculpture
by Anatol Herzfeld in Hombroich.

Embedded in a bizarre garden landscape
of box and birch: the elegant Graubner
Pavilion with its round glass bay window.

Per Kirkeby, Hoidn Wang Partner and other distinguished architects and artists.

Only ten per cent of the total area, which looks like a building exhibition on the plans, is to be built following the initiators' wishes. It emerges from Wilfried Wang's essay on the Utopian urban landscape that the search is back on for a happier connection between town and countryside, in an attempt to get away from inhospitable modern cities. • This is to be based on the late 19th-century garden city movement and the Werkbund experiments in the early 20th century. But what role can landscape still play among this collection of architectural and urban treasures? 90 per cent is to be woodland and meadows, orchards and herb gardens, the essay states. And so are we back to the modernist idea of "neutral green" and "freely flowing" landscape, of a rural, monastic garden idyll, a new Arcadia?

Immediately after the NATO conversion site was purchased, the question arose of how nature and landscape could be treated in an up-to-date way, and the apposite insight was arrived at that it can no longer be a viable strategy to eradicate traces of contemporary history or to quote traditional, idyllic guidelines from centuries past as a response

Cf. Wang, Wilfried:
"Metamorphose –
Strukturwandel"
in: www.inselhom-
broich.de (2004)

Entrance garden of the Langen Foundation. The path takes an elegant line directly through the window to the landscape, running along the shallow reflecting pool, fringed by cherry trees.

to the challenges of the present. Instead, Müller first of all saw to it that the site was "disarmed" and had the simple military buildings skilfully renovated so that they could be used for artistic and scientific purposes. Erwin Heerich enhanced the location with three iconic brick structures; in the year 2000, Eduardo Chilida's 14-metre-high concrete sculpture "Begiari," corresponding with a former military watchtower,

Tadao Ando built the new museum for the Langen Foundation, embedded in the sculpted landscape, on the site of the Hombroich missile station in 2004.

Erwin Heerich also furnished the missile station with sculptural architecture, used as research institutes. This is the Institute of Biophysics.

placed a symbol, visible for miles around, of the aesthetic and moral conversion the place had undergone. But the landscape character of the whole complex is defined only by the existing, attractive structure of metre-high, extensively planted protective walls of chippings – now reminiscent of American Land Art –, and a sparse stock of trees and bushes, some of which has emerged spontaneously.

Tadao Ando also felt committed to the bleak tendencies in the character of the landscape when in 2001 he revealed his first plans for the new Langen Foundation museum building at the missile station to the art collectors Marianne and Viktor Langen. This museum of modern Western and traditional Japanese art was opened in September 2004. The complex in exposed concrete, glass and steel fits in with the spirit of the place. It consists of two sections, protected by an existing southern earth wall, and a new northern one, and scarcely protrudes above the earthworks. Visitors first discover the northern end of the 43-metre-long Japanese gallery, which takes the form of a glazed lounge just under 3.5 metres high, and seems to float above an elegant, shallow mirror pool. Access to the lounge, to the entrance of the museum, from the street is first through the gateway in a long exposed concrete roof, curving concavely, and then along the edge of the pool, accompanied by a row of decorative Japanese cherry trees, to the Japanese building. It lies in the landscape parallel with the northern earth wall and was conceived as a long, windowless concrete core, accessible all round and surrounded with a glass skin on the outside. The second part of the museum, housing modern Western art, is a lower, U-shaped concrete structure sunk into the terrain, branching off

at an angle of 45 degrees to the more prominent Japanese building. In the Langen Foundation, earth sculpture and building sculpture combine to form an attractive, unassuming ensemble providing surprising exterior and interior experiences that fit in successfully with the Hombroich culture area, which has so far not been aesthetically overcharged.

Katsuhito Nishikawa fitted two metal bowls, like parabolic mirrors, between the concrete walls of the missile launching ramps, listening to the sky and offering shelter.

Sculptures that can be walked on and entered have evolved out of the legacy of the Cold War, like this one by Katsuhito Nishikawa between the former missile bunkers.

Tales of the water dragon

Landscape architects:
Agence Ter
Public park
Size: approx.
35 hectares
Completed for the
Regional Horticultural
Show in 2000

There were urgent warnings about climbing down into the mysterious green crater and penetrating the apparently infinite depths of the stone chasm. But the urge to get to the bottom of the causes of the mysterious eruption was simply irresistible. When the children had crossed the sunken crater garden, and finally came across a mysterious, circular sheet of calm water 18 metres underground, it was too late. An eerie sound of thunder from the underworld, flashes of lightning, and suddenly the surface of the water started to seethe in a way that boded ill. But the way back to daylight was simply too long.

The story of Aqua Magica, "Park der Magischen Wasser" in Bad Oeynhausen, started thousands of years ago, when tectonic forces shaped the face of the earth, but not just the superficial appearance of the landscape. New fault lines appeared deep down below, and salt water from their crevices that is still forcing its way to the surface today formerly served as a fluid culture medium for the region's economic growth. The first salt spring was discovered in Bad Oeynhausen in 1745, which triggered the building of salt factories and the development of a prosperous salt industry. After the therapeutic effects of thermal brine were discovered, spa operations started to be established in the East Westphalia-Lippe region in the mid-19th century. After their heyday, spa visitor numbers declined in the late 20th century, as the health service underwent its structural crisis; the many health centres and spa clinics were less and less well used, and the decision was taken to give the region a boost with the 2000 Horticultural Show.

The Parisian landscape architects Agence Ter won a planning competition in 1997. The aim of Henri Bava's and Olivier Philippe's "Aqua Magica" design for the 35-hectare site between the towns of Bad Oeynhausen and Löhne aimed to make the two invisible fault lines and the force of the underground water open to sensual experience – using dispersed stone bands, a global climate avenue, secret flower gardens and gardens with fountains and water.

The water crater that still enchants visitors even years after the horticultural show ended is a central feature of the park. A path over a treeless meadow suddenly takes them to the edge of the circular earth crater that is skilfully positioned on a rise; its walls are planted with low willows in different shades of green. The three-metre-high, bush-like serviceberries that cover the bottom of the hollow uniformly do not thrust up above the edge of the crater, which deliberately changes the sense of scale. It is impossible to avoid the impression of seeing the bottom of an extensive landscape crater over the tops of large trees.

The bottom of the earth crater is green in summer, and the low canopy gives an extraordinary sense of space.

In the middle, the tree canopy has a huge-looking crater pot towering above it, whose rust-red Corten steel walls stand out strongly from their green surroundings. Two narrow entrances, closed by heavy steel doors, promise access to the water crater. Inside it is clad with wire ballast baskets reminiscent of the insulating fireclay lining in firing furnaces.

Curiosity is aroused: what threatening dinosaur is confined behind these thick walls at the bottom of the lost world in the crater? A steep staircase or a hidden ramp leads to the floor of the earth crater, plunging first into a sunken, still garden world. The serviceberries grow between long, narrow bands of concrete that circle the crater in the formation of floating tree-trunks. Alternating plantations of fern and shade-loving perennials form a rich, green carpet that is crossed on concrete strips, almost like walking a tightrope, until finally you pass through one of the great steel doors and step onto the steel platform framing the central aperture.

Water drips from the gabion walls of the shaft onto the steel spiral staircase and on down into the shadowy realms at the bottom of the shaft. The sound of dripping water echoes from the depths.

Only two narrow entrances give a glimpse inside the water crater.

Peace still reigns in the pool at the bottom of the crater in the Park of Magic Waters.

Down there, on the lowest platform, children stand at the rails. They stare down in fascination at the circular expanse of black water, which suddenly seems to explode: a foaming column of water one and a half metres wide shoots and seethes up the shaft towards the light, over the edge of the crater and into the sky. Suddenly it collapses again, enveloping the children and everything around them in dense water vapour that the rays of the sun suddenly penetrate and set aglow.

This spectacle, perfectly staged technically in terms of water, light and sound, is repeated at unexpected intervals, in different rhythms and degrees of intensity. It delights the amazed spectators and triggers powerful visual associations: all round the water crater, in the peaceful shade of the idyllic grove of serviceberries, through which a breath of water occasionally wafts, stories of geysers in faraway regions of the world come to mind, of volcanic eruptions, dragon fountains in famous Baroque gardens, spouting whales, deep wells in the desert and magic springs in countless fairy tales.

The steel circle whose interior walls are lined with gabions tower over the canopy of a grove of serviceberries.

"Gardens, parks and squares should tell us about their history, but they should also tell new stories. They are poetic places of our past, present and future," Zurich landscape architect Dieter Kienast once wrote, thus formulating one of the most important criteria for designing good gardens.

Agence Ter's sunken garden with water crater in Bad Oeynhausen does not just tell, in a restricted space, a story about the magic of the underground water to which a whole region owes its identity; it also displays great knowledge of aesthetics and garden and landscape architecture. The garden architects use archetypal garden and landscape elements like the circular crater, the secluded grove, the *hortus conclusus,* the abyss of hell, the deep well-shaft and the wild fountain to invoke ancient ideal images, and tempt visitors to take their thoughts back to the gardens where the storytellers put their listeners under their spell.

But shortly afterwards a powerful jet of water shoots 35 metres up out of the Corten steel container.

When sunlight meets the water vapour rising from below it shimmers in all the colours of the rainbow.

Dripping wet walls as evidence of the last eruption.

Leaves and blossom glow in front of the dark red Corten steel wall.

Tree island and woodland clearing

In 18th-century London, and in other cities in England and Scotland, the squares were among the most important public green spaces in prosperous urban districts. These attractive garden islands started to come into being in the late 17th century. They were planted with selected tree and shrub varieties, and lovingly tended by the residents. This prestigious "green centre," a mixture of square and park, soon caught on in Europe and North America, and is still cited as a planning model for district parks, as in the case of the new, grid-like "Expo Estate" on the Kronsberg, 106 metres high, near Hanover. But are these centuries-old models, created for prestige purposes, still valid for the 21st century?

The Hanover landscape architects Irene Lohaus and Peter Carl drew on the English model when planning their North and Centre district parks in 1996, because they thought the respective areas of just under 1 and 1.4 hectares were too large for squares and too small for parks. And also the new parks – just like their old English predecessors – were intended to convey a certain intimacy and have a strong enough character of their own to give the residents a sense of local identity. Two opposite concepts characterize the two parks. A large rounded oval of woodland, set in a stone area of approximately square size, is the chief feature of the North district park. In contrast with this, the somewhat larger Centre district park appears as a clearing with a slightly twisted square ground plan, punched out of a densely planted grove of whitebeams.

Something that made planning difficult but makes the realized projects all the more interesting is the fact that both sites slope westwards by five per cent. The 1.5-metre-high earth oval in the Centre district park, planted with pines and grass, turned out to be an intelligent trick here. Instead of levelling the whole area, the hourglass-shaped

Landscape architects:
Irene Lohaus and Peter Carl
Public parks
Size: 1 and 1.4 hectares
Completed in 1996 – 2000

A small, circular pinewood, set in a sloping, approximately square area, gives the North district park in Kronsberg, Hanover its distinctive character.

Looking against the evening sun into the little pinewood from the wisteria-covered steel pergola on the top edge of the park.

The concrete block cuboids set into the square horizontally as structuring elements and seating show clearly how the terrain slopes.

body of earth creates a range of different terrain dispositions and possible uses. Where the pine grove ends up in an almost flat area, a long "play band" was created, with sandy surface and a collection of popular playground equipment for the children.

The landscape architects also paid a lot of attention to the corner of the square, which inevitably turned out a little too large because of the circle that has been superimposed in the centre. Following the slope, the area is sparsely planted with shrubs and oleasters and paved with bands of different widths of large-format concrete slabs; green joints three centimetres wide have been created between them in the longitudinal direction to allow rainwater to seep away.

From time to time solid concrete beams thrust out horizontally from the slab bands and the slope, serving mainly as seating. But above all they accentuate the topography and leave behind wide trails of lime-

Only the long play area crosses the pine plantation, structuring the circle of green, creating space for games and the children to play.

The attractive character of the park design also derives from the compelling details.

Simple ramps lead from the raised frame to the central grassy area in the Centre district park.

stone ballast, where a variety of spontaneous vegetation has sprung up, as it also has in the green joints. Rainwater is captured in blind drains at the foot of the slope and then drips into an underground "sound-space." In contrast with this empathetic acoustic experiment on the western edge, the eastern boundary of the square, a long pergola in Corten steel, intended to have wisteria growing on it, looks rather more modish.

The borders of the Centre district park consist of a trimmed hornbeam hedge, which is not particularly spectacular, but all the more convincing for that. The grove of whitebeams make a powerful impression, planted in a tight grid about four metres apart. The artwork added in 1999 – "(4x) 28 Words" – by Dieter Froelich, a series of inscribed stone tablets laid in the shade of the grove, does not make a spatial impact, but accentuates the place unostentatiously. The border between the

Steps running all round the
park provide seating.

A transparent fence in the lower part
of the park separates the areas belonging
to the adjacent kindergarten.

Dieter Froelich's "(4x) 28 Worte"
comment on the view across the
terraced area of the park.

Curved bands of Corten steel shore up
the shallow grassy terraces that constantly
blend into each other.

dense grove and the central clearing is additionally reinforced by the
fact that the inner lawn surface is sunk by one metre.

Steps running all the way round and inserted ramps lead from the
water-bound framing area into the inside of the park. Here steel bands
running along the contours create even, usable lawn terraces with
individual decorative apple trees, playground equipment and mobile
seating. The competition design for the park had originally included a
children's day-care centre on the northern edge of the clearing, which
would have shared use of the whole park area, but the responsible
authorities were unable to accept this idea. The architects Heerwagen
Lohmann Uffelmann built a simple, two-storey playschool on the north-
western edge of the clearing, but fenced off an area for the children
that was allegedly easier to supervise; fortunately this scarcely im-
pinges on the generosity of the overall concept for the park.

Unlike the English squares, the two parks in Kronsberg are not just pret-
ty green oases, but usable urban open spaces. Here we come across two
of the most important archetypes in the history of the cultural landscape: tree island and woodland clearing. The power of these landscape archetypes, paired with today's high-quality open space design,
gives the two new parks an unmistakable, almost poetic character.

Iceberg in a sea of lilac

Landscape architect:
Yves Brunier
Public square
Size: approx. 4,000 m²
Completed in 1989 – 1992

In hot summers, when the crape myrtle does full justice to its reputation as the "lilac of the south" and over 50 Lagerstroemia indica spread their purply-pink umbrella of blossom over the Place du Général Leclerc, it is easy to forget that you are in the station square in Tours. Rushing water can be heard in the centre of the square, the sound it makes drowns the noise of the traffic that does not just run round the square but parks underneath it as well. If you sit down on one of the many benches in the shade of the small, picturesque flowering trees, then the hedge of severely trimmed yew trees about one and a half metres high that runs round the edges of the square cuts the traffic out visually as well. Even the ventilation shafts for the underground car park disappear in the dark yews.

The illusion of a lilac garden in the middle of the city could be perfect if there were a carpet of grass or perennials on the ground. Instead of this, the little, gnarled tree-trunks with their smooth grey bark grow out of a homogeneous granite surface, and a broad pathway runs diagonally across the grid-like planting of the grove, linking the two large urban focal points: the old, stately station building in the south and the futuristic, streamlined Le Vinci congress centre in the north.

The Place du Général Leclerc owes its new design to an architectural competition for the new Centre international des Congrès Le Vinci and

Jean Nouvel's Centre international des Congrès Le Vinci rises like a stylish luxury yacht between the crape myrtles behind Yves Brunier's fountain.

a car park under the adjacent square in 1989. The young French landscape architect Yves Brunier, a member of Jean Nouvel's successful competition team, developed the new urban identity of the square. After Nouvel had won the competition and been commissioned to build the congress centre, the city decided to commission the design for the square separately from Yves Brunier and his partner, the landscape architect Isabelle Auricoste. After a three year planning and building period the remarkable project was completed in 1992, but too late for Yves Brunier, who died of Aids in 1991 at the age of 29.

Brunier, who started his meteoric career in Rem Koolhaas's OMA practice after studying in Paris, was not looking for harmonious natural images in the city. His designs were much more inclined to cultivate a

Strictly trimmed, dark yew hedges frame the square powerfully.

creative strategy in which the apparent contradictions of everyday urban life, the breaks between nature and culture, fused to create new connections and meanings. This method was never expressed so clearly as in Brunier's pictorial collages, which he used to express the character of his planned landscape interventions with complete precision.

Like his collages, even though without the virtuosity of his experiments on paper, Brunier's concepts usually consisted conceptionally of fragments from different images, situations or ideas which he brought together in refreshingly unconventional compositions, without the individual elements losing their identity. Brunier's works thus reflected an inner turmoil and a state of uncertainty that was not only typical of his life, but did characterize modern society's actual sense of life.

The Place du Général Leclerc is both a puzzle picture and a collage. Everything from the trees to the benches is firmly anchored in a complete granite covering on a grid structure. Even the direct lateral path connecting the station and the nearby park is separated from the actual square by a yew hedge and fringed with magnolias in a linear row. The area only becomes a hybrid between public square and garden through the combination of controlled urban hardness and extravagant blossom.

The water-cooled glass body of the fountain seems almost icy in contrast with the "lilac of the south."

The collage-like nature of the project can be seen at the central design element, the fountain. Brunier placed a large fountain about 23 metres long in the diagonal pathway between the glazed façades of the congress building and the terminus station. The fountain's almond-shaped ground plan seems like an obstinate foreign body in the general plan, pulling out of the orderly pattern.

The fountain is also an opening providing light for the underground car park. A striking bluish-green glass object is placed over this aperture, closing the skylight like a ship's hull that has tipped over.

Powerful jets of water shoot out of a whole battery of nozzles all round the body of glass, washing and cooling it. Seen from the underground car park, it looks as though a river is streaming across the roof. An impressive show, if it were not for the massive support structure for the glass body, which considerably mars the effect.

"Glacis d'eau" was Yves Brunier's note on his watercolour sketch for the project, wanting to see a green iceberg in the middle of the square. The icy colour of the glass body, the cool air and the mighty rushing sound determine the atmosphere around the fountain. In the middle of the red-glowing sea of blossom provided by the sun-starved Lagerstroemia the bluish water-feature seems even icier, and the contrast with its surroundings even stronger. As a backdrop to the foam, Jean Nouvel's building suddenly looks like the bridge of a modern luxury liner thrusting into the square.

At night, the flowing character of the Place du Général Leclerc is determined by gentle, indirect lighting. Then the fountain is illuminated from inside and lurks in the centre of the square like a heavy, fluorescent creature, luring nocturnal revellers with its magic light. Only the colourful neon signs above the treetops signal the city's vibrant nightlife.

Backlit, a sparkling carpet of water pours over the vault of the glass dome.

The dense stand of small Lagerstroemia indica with its gnarled trunks gives the urban square an intimate atmosphere.

Yves Brunier developed new spatial and recreational qualities between the glazed façades of the new congress building and the old Lyon terminus station.

Lit from inside at night, the fountain lurks in the middle of the square like a giant fluorescent organism.

Box-trees parking in Stock Exchange Square

Landscape architect:
Alexandre Chemetoff
Public square
Size: 2,100 m²
Completed in 1993

When Napoleon III officially opened the Palais du Commerce in Lyon in August 1860, this magnificent building, designed by René Dardel, was seen as a symbol of the hoped-for success of imperial-liberal economic policies. In order for the opulently decorated north façade of the building to achieve the right effect, a small square was created in front of it in the dense structure of the city, the Place de la Bourse – Stock Exchange Square. When the commercial and banking town hit another phase of economic stagnation over a hundred years later as result of the 1991 Gulf War, this had serious consequences for the image of the city as a whole, not just the Place de la Bourse: the pause in the building boom was used to draw up the "Lyon 2010" development plan in 1992. This was intended to make the city more attractive, but without impairing its existing urban and architectural qualities.

Redesigning and refurbishing the inner city open spaces was among the most important measures, alongside the plan for dealing with the riverside and the floodlighting plan. Many of the squares that had once been so attractive, like the Place de la République, the Place Antonin Poncet, the Place des Terreaux or the Place de Célestine, and also the Rue de la République pedestrian area had now – as in most large European cities – become desolate car parks.

It would not have been possible to design any of the squares that are now such attractive features of central Lyon appropriately if parked cars had not been banished underground. This meant that central underground parking had to be found for over 3000 cars, and even here architectural design was seen as very important. In the Place de Célestine, prestigiously transformed by the landscape architects Michel Desvigne and Christine Dalnoky, visitors can now use Daniel Buren's periscope to take an interesting look into the underworld, and the view is definitely not just of functionally lit parking spaces.

Just a few years after realization the Place de la Bourse in Lyon seems lavishly green.

There are also 560 parking spaces under the Place de la Bourse, a project by the French landscape architect Alexandre Chemetoff. 126 box trees, trimmed as spheres in overlarge clay pots, are "parked" in the square in seven parallel rows between the Rue de la Bourse and the Rue de la République. The pots are automatically watered from openings in the ground, clearly signalling that that no soil has developed naturally under the surface of this inner-city square.

This acceptance of the urban character of open spaces and the refusal to use superficially decorative imitations of nature to camouflage technical structures underground is a characteristic of all the new squares in Lyon. With the exception of the Place de la Bourse, no attempt was made to introduce intensive green planting to the refur-

126 box trees in overlarge clay pots create a highly individual sense of proportion.

Opulent pot plants in front of the magnificent façade of the Palais du Commerce.

"Box parade," structured on the ground by the ventilation slits for the underground car park.

A simple natural stone block as a fountain and gently splashing introduction to the green city square.

bished urban spaces. This means that the characteristic spatial proportions and the magnificent façades make a particular impact. In contrast with the dense urban spaces, the green areas of the city, the trees fringing the riverbanks and the park landscape beneath the cathedral make a particularly powerful effect.

In the same way, the Place de la Bourse also makes an effect in the texture of its reticently planted surroundings of being a valuable, surprisingly green island of peace in the city centre. A gently bubbling fountain, realized as a solid block of granite, was placed on the granite-paved surface of the square at the edge of the quieter Rue de la Bourse. The square surface of its water reflects lively light patterns into the tops of the sycamores. Trees grow only on the northern edge of the square, where appropriately dimensioned plant troughs were built in when the underground car park was being built. Chemetoff thinks it is important to stagger plants according to their height so that they do not cover up the façade of the Chamber of Commerce. Low-growing serviceberries and trimmed cherry laurel hedges were planted in linear beds. The freely growing crowns of the trees form a stark contrast with the austerely

In 1994, the Place de la Bourse still seemed relatively open.

trimmed box trees and bands of hedge. Niches are let into these from time to time, with park benches inviting passers-by to sit down.

When night falls in Lyon we can see how successfully the illumination plan has been implemented: harsh shop-window lighting has been abandoned in the city's finest squares in favour of discreet, precisely focused illumination for the magnificent façades. In the Place de la Bourse the show side of René Dardel's magnificent building glows in muted light, and ground-recessed luminaries in the square light the green atmospherically.

The trimmed box spheres have gained in precision with age, but also in character.

It is especially due to the efficacious cooperation of architects, landscape architects, artists and engineers that the inner-city "mission presqu'île" was so successful in the historic centre. Today Lyon is seen throughout the world as a model for skilful inner-city open space design.

Just under ten years after its inauguration the square seems to be almost overwhelmed by green.

Fragments of garden history

Landscape architect:
Kathryn Gustafson
Public park
Size: approx. 6 hectares
Completed in 1995

The little town of Terrasson-la-Villedieu in the French Périgord, picturesquely set in the Vézère valley, shifted into the spotlight of tourist interest in the mid-nineties with a new garden attraction. According to the regional tourist association, Les Jardins de l'Imaginaire, along with three classical gardens, make up the "quatres jardins exceptionnels en Dordogne."

The American landscape architect Kathryn Gustafson drew on the rich horticultural repertoire of earlier centuries for her park concept: when Terrasson announced a competition for a landscaped park on a slope above the town in the early nineties, the initiators were looking for a garden to link the finesse of famous Italian Renaissance gardens with the grandeur of legendary French Baroque parks and the timeless elegance of Japanese meditation gardens.

Already in the competition plan with its elegant basic forms flowing like a design for textile folds it became clear that Gustafson was not trying for a serial accumulation of single historical motifs. She was in fact designing a kind of *Gesamtkunstwerk,* and embedding it in the topography, which was modelled sculpturally to an extent. She covered the steep slope with gently undulating terraces and planted them with monochrome perennials and grasses. From a distance the relief is reminiscent of ploughed furrows and thus also of the former agricultural use to which the terrain had been put.

The main pathway in the park runs like a narrative thread up the slope through an oak forest and open meadows. A potpourri of design accessories, from the golden Ariadne's thread Fil d'or in the trees to the great wind games along the Axe des vents or little bells in the oak trees of the Bois sacré, are intended to enhance the importance of the garden and pictorial sequences.

The route from the little town of Terrasson-la-Villedieu leads out of the valley and up into the Jardins de l'Imaginaire.

The view down in to the Vézère valley is over gently undulating grassy slopes planted with lavender.

Water – the elixir of life in any garden – plays a key role throughout the park, telling stories from all epochs of garden culture. Sometimes it provides an apparently endless, Baroque-looking water axis, then again – at the southernmost point of the park – it enlivens a flower-bed with water reminiscent of classical Renaissance gardens in which the watercourse was central, as a symbol of life. In historical models the live-giving element ideally came from a spring in a mysterious grotto, but the river in the Jardins de l'Imaginaire rises somewhere on the edge of the wood and flows over an architecturally designed water staircase between blue shrubs offering blossom and fragrance and down into the Forêt des jets. Here a whole forest of fountains shoot up into the air; a magical motif that was presented in a masterly fashion above all in the Mannerist gardens of the Renaissance.

In the famous 16th and 17th-century gardens the water usually reached the end of its course in a magnificent flowerbed with water or a large, calm mirror of water, symbolizing the sea, and at the same time the end of life's pathway. In Gustafson's garden it ends suddenly in a concrete reservoir on the lowest terrace of the garden. Only a few paces away is the steel pergola of the Roseraie, a space surrounded by climbing roses, covering an area of about 1,000 square metres. This structure too is adapted to the topography and looks like a magic carpet of flowers under which visitors can enjoy the fragrant shade.

The flowing river motif crops up once more, but this time in a way that is intelligible to people who are less well versed in the history of garden art. The landscape architect devotes a little fountain to each of the

The earth formations are also reminiscent of the former agricultural use of the cultural landscape.

An axis marked out with wind games links the gardens with Terrasson visually.

Visitors stroll through the oak wood
along the Fil d'or to the next,
open garden space.

The Théâtre de verdure, an open-air
theatre, welcomes visitors in
a crescent-shaped clearing.

Simple, elegantly curved benches in
black-painted steel reflect the daylight
and also the mysterious, crescent-shaped
lake that visitors seem to see.

Seen from this perspective, the mirror surface turns out to be a glass roof.

Inside the greenhouse are light-flooded spaces for events and exhibitions.

Ian Ritchie's greenhouse sits proudly on the topmost slope of the garden like a great bastion built from gabions.

Next two pages:
A whole forest of fountains shoots water up into the air in the water-garden with its Forêt des jets, washed about with the scent of blossom.

earth's great rivers, the Euphrates, the Nile, the Ganges, the Mississippi and the Amazon, arranged along the paths through the Bois sacré. A river delta has been engraved on each of five stone slabs. Here too a little water runs through the incised grooves, enlivening the ramifications of the graphic.

When looking at the slope in the park from a distance a somewhat amazing sight seems to greet us: a crescent-shaped reservoir lake that has turned to ice. But in fact this is the sweeping span of the greenhouse, designed by the architect Ian Ritchie. If it were not for the fact that the canal and railings prevent us from walking on the roof the illusion would be perfect. The massive walls of the building were constructed from gabions that are reminiscent of the traditional drystone masonry in terraced vineyards, and also make the building look like a massive erratic block. Its powerful exterior, thrusting out from the slope, contrasts attractively with the light-flooded interior of the orangery, where citrus plants exude their fragrance. The shape of the roof is reflected above the building in the Théâtre de verdure, the open-air theatre that is moulded into the slope as a half-moon clearing and furnished with simple, elegantly curving benches in black-painted steel.

"The gardens of the world cannot be bought. But we can explain them," said Kathryn Gustafson about her ambitious design. But ultimately the "Gardens of the Imagination" explain only themselves. The rest is left to the imagination, and that is good.

A carpet of blossom providing fragrant shade covers the steel pergola.

An apparently endless, Baroque-looking water table draws a hard horizontal line on the garden landscape.

The shade of fragrant roses makes it particularly pleasant to spend time in the rose garden.

The peaceful garden Utopia

Landscape architects:
Vogt Landschafts-
architekten
Temporary public
garden
Size: approx. 5,000 m²
Completed in 2002 for
the Swiss National
Exhibition EXPO.02

"Inflicting and suffering violence. Openly or covertly, furtively even. To disturb, destroy, ill-treat, repress. There are countless forms, causes and effects of violence, especially as an everyday occurrence. But they have one thing in common – they all have victims. Even when we think that violence can be explained as inevitable, or justified as a deterrent or as defence. Is it possible to make people aware of these problems, even to exhibit them? How can moments of contact be introduced that resist their becoming accustomed to them? Many images have lost their power to move." • Exhibition director Eva Afuhs, and Martin Heller, artistic director of the Swiss National Exhibition EXPO.02, sensed how difficult it would be to express the omnipresent phenomenon of violence strikingly as part of a temporary garden on the outskirts of the old town in Murten. Even so the International Committee of the Red Cross, the Swiss Red Cross and the Avina Foundation decided to realize this exhibition project.

Afuhs, Eva, Heller,
Martin: "Spuren der
Gewalt" in: SRK –
Schweizerisches Rotes
Kreuz (ed.): Garten der
Gewalt. Jardin de la
violence. Giardino
della violenza. Bern
2002; p.7

During the intensive preliminary discussions for the spectacular EXPO.02 it also quickly became clear to the team of landscape architects under the direction of Günther Vogt that any attempt to set up symbolic presentations of violence in a garden would be doomed to inevitable failure in the face of the scenes of real violence that are present every day. And so Vogt Landschaftsarchitekten used the attractive sloping site around the local museum, a restored historical mill, to create an ambitiously designed, terraced park. They seem to have left the task of actually coming to terms with the proposed theme of violence to a group of fine artists who made a considerable effort to convey the horrors of violence effectively in individual installations, in-

A wooden bridge, with a view of the Lac de Morat in the background, leads from the garden to the top floor of the old mill.

cluding sound and light installations, hoardings, showcases and a kind of "aggression course" with instructions for gestural provocations to violence. But it would probably have needed other, perhaps more decisive interventions even to come close to expressing the horrors of violence effectively, but this would probably have completely spoiled the EXPO.02 visitors' cheerful exhibition mood – think for example of the shocking exhibits by the British artist Damien Hirst.

"The garden that presents itself as a perfect world is a Utopia, a place that does not exist," was Günther Vogt's apposite remark, questioning ideal notions of the garden as an image of the earthly paradise that was once lost, • but to which many garden-lovers still stubbornly cling to. In his temporary project by Lake Neuenburg, his sceptical attitude to idealized garden images could be read in numerous subtle discrepancies that were consistently to be found in the park. For example, the slope with its terraced lawns looked like a gentle green carpet from

Vogt, Günther:
"Der Garten der
Gewalt" in: SRK –
Schweizerisches
Rotes Kreuz (ed.):
Garten der Gewalt.
Jardin de la violence.
Giardino della
violenza. Bern 2002;
p.30

the highest point on the site. But from the foot of the slope the picture was dominated by pitch-black industrial conveyor belts: the supporting walls of the numerous steps had been clad in this artificial hard rubber material, apparently forcing the terraces into robust, unyielding fetters.

Two small cream-coloured pavilions in the densely wooded parts of the park were equally disturbing. From a distance they looked light and inviting, but on closer examination they turned out to be solid blocks of wax into which sensitive natural materials like peacocks' feathers, fresh fern fronds and fragile snail-shells had been inserted, so that they were preserved in questionable, eternally youthful beauty.

The sloping site behind the local museum in Murten was temporarily converted into an expressive terraced landscape.

The garden ensemble of terraced lawns, tree ferns and olive trees seems strangely exotic, but also attractive.

The cold block of ice in the garden turns out to be a little wax house, opaque, closed, unfathomable.

The traditional garden arbour provided a model for the little, seemingly monolithic wax houses, melting into the birch grove.

Even the trunks of young birch trees in the freshly planted, unduly dense grove east of the old mill had obviously been forced into wax blocks and seemed to be tied violently into a corset. Wax was also the basic material used to make a fountain and a little stream in the form of water-steps. What if the cooling water were to stop flowing? Would the heat-sensitive material become distorted in the summer heat, would the streambed and the fountain melt and thus be destroyed? Solid and yet pliable at the same time, the wax created

highlights in the "Garten der Gewalt" that were as ambivalent as they were attractive.

The landscape architects wanted to create additional disturbances by planting exotic trees intended to spoil the sense of homely familiarity: gnarled olive trees in traditional farmhouse-style vegetable and herb beds, or exotic tree-ferns in the middle of carpets of native ferns. But most of the visitors to the park simply did not notice these subtle disturbances in their EXPO.02 enthusiasm. The public were astonished by a historic fountain near the mill that had been provided with a new edge for its pool: the old fountain seemed to be drowning in its own water, and could only be made out as a pale and ghostly presence

Sharp contrasts between the white of the densely planted, slender birch trunks and the black rubber of the supporting walls are the key features of the image.

The water-steps, here articulating the sloping site, find their traditional models in the history of classical garden art.

Soft wax, bandaged with hard rubber, forms a little water-course.

The old fountain by the mill, drowned in its own water, seems strangely morbid and yet beautiful.

under the new surface. Where the images of subtle violence ingeniously created by landscape architecture were so refined that they did not disturb the general impression of untroubled garden beauty to any noticeable extent, artistically staged cries of aggression from a flowerbed, triggered by a light barrier, not only seemed interchangeable, but also markedly overstaged and ultimately almost ridiculous. The Garden of Violence did not intend to present itself either as a spectacle or as a plea, but rather to heighten awareness that violence is an everyday component of the world around us that can only be discerned by paying sensitive attention and perhaps brought under control in this way. This conceptual balancing act could hardly be brought off successfully. Any garden, however like paradise it may seem, any landscape that still seems momentarily Arcadian, can become a scene of brutal violence in no time. It is precisely these breaks that occur so very suddenly in an apparently perfect world that makes such devastating effect. Many of the cultural landscapes that seem so attractive today, like the Vietnamese rice fields, for example, were not only the scenes of brutal acts of war, but are partly – as can be seen from the example of German moor landscape cultivated by forced labour – the direct result of brutal violence by man against man. The persistence in

The ferns grow hesitantly out of the shady little valley towards the harsh sunlight.

seeing gardens and landscapes as symbols of a peaceful life and cultivated nature is due to an effective human suppression mechanism. The garden as a perfect world is – considered rationally – actually a Utopia, and yet we love the idea of the garden as an earthly paradise where violence is powerless.

A breath of emphatically subtropical exoticism in the middle of Switzerland wafts around the forest of tree ferns.

Empty plinths in the box parterre

Landscape architects:
Kienast Vogt Partner / Vogt
Landschaftsarchitekten
Private park
Size: 2.3 hectares
Completed in 1996–2000

If you had visited the industrial magnate Carl Martin Leonhard Bodmer and his wife Anna Vogel at their Rüschlikon country seat in the middle of the last century, you would have turned off from the main road into an avenue and let the limes trees guide you down the slope into the shady courtyard, surrounded by luxuriant conifers, in front of the portal of the upper-class, Neo-baroque villa. Once the front door and finally even the large doors leading from the beautiful salon to the sunny garden terrace had been opened to you, you could look between two trees over the flanking box parterre with roses and on to the central part of the garden: a generous, square carpet of lawn, framed at the sides by two chestnut avenues, a fountain on the central axis, and stretching behind it the picturesque Alpine panorama on the horizon. The tree-framed square of lawn dating from the twenties is still the heart of the garden as a whole, but the fountain has disappeared, and so has the view of the Alps, which is blocked by a sweep of large maple trees.

Now as 80 years ago, the villa on the Bodmer estate is the key feature of the centre of the park in Rüschlikon. In the foreground is a sculpture by Ulrich Rückriem.

Anyone looking for Swiss Re's new, generously conceived Centre for Global Dialogue today will tend to pass the avenue to the former Bodmer estate without noticing it and not leave the road until the point where small groups of trees and shaped hedges mark the drive to the elegant seminar building by the architects Meili & Peter. Its stylistic reticence could scarcely provide a greater contrast with the nearby villa, built in 1926/27 by the architects Richard von Sinner and Hans Beyeler in the historical style of 18th-century Bernese country houses. Framed by new architectural statements, the old villa seems like a valuable jewel-case whose costliness is ostentatiously underlined by the noble gold-leaf finish for the window-frames. But the thing that links old and new most clearly is the villa garden, assumed to have been designed by the garden architect Vivell, which always combined architecturally formal French garden elements with freely landscaped garden areas in the English style, forming a charming contrast. Current design features were skilfully added as part of the new building and conversion programme, planned between 1996 and 1998 by the Zurich landscape architects Kienast Vogt Partner, and realized by the year 2000 by Vogt Landschaftsarchitekten.

The characteristics of the new garden design are respect for the historical design concept, discreet accentuation of the existing park elements and a tactful reinterpretation of those parts of the garden that had not stood the test of time or had not survived the most recent building work. For example, new planting reinforced the picturesque group of pines on the grassy knoll by the new main entrance, reached

Set above Lake Zurich, the park has always benefited from the splendid view, here towards the northern end of the lake.

The view of Lake Zurich can be enjoyed from the sun terrace, and in clear weather the nearby Alpine panorama can be seen as well.

Next two pages:
View from the villa over the box parterre between rows of old chestnuts with a rectangular water-table as a central accent.

The shady corridor leads past the redesigned box parterre, linking the old villa and the new seminar centre.

by a narrow, twisty park path. At the top of the hill, which the conference centre crosses horizontally like a luxury liner cutting through an ocean wave, there is nothing to suggest the central garden space at a lower level. A minimalist sculpture by Sol LeWitt has anchored itself into the hill in a comb shape, and draws the eye down to Lake Zurich. It is only by the metre-high retaining wall further down that it is possible to look over the two box parterres with the empty plinths in the centre. The statuettes were in poor condition and could not be restored, but instead of reconstructing them the plinths were left empty, which gave the rectangular parterres a new, non-architectural look. Different varieties of box in various shades of green draw mysteriously amorphous shapes, and one tries in vain to relate them to the formerly Neo-baroque gardens. The attractive and unusual game with colours and shapes around the empty plinths captivates viewers. The unaffectedly contemporary interpretation of historical garden art elements intelligently sets new and attractive trends.

Two long reflecting pools were also created on former ground plans. These are modern mirror surfaces, apparently set in the ground without frames. They reflect atmospheric light into the shady green of the old chestnut avenues, and mirror the disturbing emptiness of the plinths in the box parterres. The western pool leads to the key point at which the seminar building thrusts through the chestnuts towards the central green space, as if connecting with the heart of the park like a spatial joint. The large, glazed seminar room on the protruding top floor enjoys a view over the treetops and down to the lawn, which in spring is intended to be transformed into a colourful carpet of blossom by 400,000 crocuses – a welcome change in the midst of the largely monochrome setting in finely graded shades of green and different leaf textures. On the ground floor, the enjoyable sense of facing the garden succeeds only at the interface between old and new, at the glass façade of the library. This opens up to the east on to the tree-hall where the fountain used to be the visual focus. Ulrich Rückriem accentuated this place with a flat and ground-recessed powerful natural stone sculpture that contrasts in carefully nuanced colours with the gravel pavement.

On the Lake Zurich side, the large viewing terrace provides topographical emphasis for the edge of the slope. Two striking groups of three Lombardy poplars will continue to frame the magnificent view over the countryside on the shores of Lake Zurich. Timber that blocked the view has been cut down, and the slope planted instead with an ingenious composition of flowering shrubs and herbaceous perennials intended to provide variety throughout the year.

On the projecting piece of terrain facing south-east and Lake Zurich, the architects built a teahouse that is scarcely visible from the terrace.

Large areas of window bring the lush green of the treetops into the interior of the modern seminar building.

The pools of water lie between the rows of chestnuts like large, frameless mirrors, flanked by new architectural elements.

A little below the park, a path parallel with the slope leads through lavishly mixed planting to the teahouse, emphasized by three Lombardy poplars.

The new seminar building by architects Meili & Peter thrusts out into the old park and provides a wonderful view of the surrounding trees.

Different kinds of box in varying shades of green, square-cut limes and old horse chestnuts join to create a new garden ensemble.

A broad flight of steps, flanked by trimmed lime trees, leads to the centre of the park from the villa.

Yesterday as today, a generous lawn framed by massive backdrops of trees dominates the heart of the old park.

Sol LeWitt's minimalist concrete sculpture digs into the hill like a comb, pointing deep into the Alpine landscape.

The old drive to the Bodmer villa, fringed by an avenue of limes, now plays a subsidiary role.

It has its own viewing terrace, reached by narrow steps or via the panoramic path through the flowering shrubs that runs parallel with the slope. From the teahouse, the path takes you back and up to the former gardener's house on the main road. Here again the architectural past and present meet in the tightest possible space, appositely heightened by expressive groups of trees.

The respectful, finely balanced interplay between the historical building stock and new architecture, between old garden art and modern landscape architecture, but above all the empathetic conversation between architecture, landscape architecture and fine art makes the Centre for Global Dialogue into a successful artistic ensemble. The many functional demands made by a modern seminar centre are built into the prestigious overall project apparently effortlessly, and with the required generosity of scope. Setting new trends in evolved cultural landscapes without destroying the places' existing identities is now one of the most common but also the most difficult tasks in current architecture and landscape architecture. Successful interventions stand out in many cases by combining old and new to make new connections in terms of meaning, without destroying each other's expressiveness.

An urban garden beyond ecological clichés

Landscape architects:
Kienast Vogt Partner
Private garden for
an office building
Size: 300 m²
Completed in 1995–1996

The Swiss landscape architect Dieter Kienast, one of the great names in recent European landscape architecture, never considered it beneath him to design small spaces. In this he followed Hugo von Hofmannsthal's maxim: "Whether a garden is large or small is not important. As far as possibly being beautiful is concerned, its extent matters as little as it matters whether a picture is large or small, whether a poem has ten lines or a hundred. The possibilities of being beautiful that can emerge in a square surrounded by four walls are simply immeasurable." • It is, indeed, equally as difficult to make a poem of just a few lines, a picture with just a few brushstrokes, expressive and meaningful as it is to transform a garden into a special place using simple forms and few media – and especially when it has to be created in a public urban space, and not in an intimate atmosphere of private seclusion, thus requiring a certain robustness. Simplicity is often confused with merely functional and rational design, with the result that open spaces are often banal. This is just as erroneous as top-heavy design in the interest of supposed "cosiness" or "liveliness." Simplicity and reduction do not just mean doing without the unnecessary, but also seeking universality and cultivating common things.

Dieter Kienast's extensive œuvre follows a whole range of such important principles, above all as far as handling urban greenery is concerned: "Our work is a search for urban nature in colours that can be grey as well as green," is the first of his ten theses on landscape architecture. • Marked interest in urban development and a special feel for architecture were particular features of the work of this Zurich landscape architect, who died in 1998.

The little garden for the Ernst Basler + Partner engineering practice in central Zurich is also the result of successful interdisciplinary co-operation, in this case with the Zurich architects Romero and Schaefle, who skilfully converted a former apartment block into offices. Six-storey residential and office buildings typify the front part of Mühlebachstrasse near Stadelhofen station. Most of the front gardens of the former ground floor areas of prestigious town houses have been turned into car parks. So the idea of establishing a front garden in the street space again was not fundamentally new, and yet extraordinary given the context. The remarkable character of the little garden also arises from the successful combination of compelling design and intelligent awareness of the environment, without producing rustic eco-design.

Since it has been redeveloped, the whole front garden area is in the form of a 50-cm-high, steel drawer, thrusting out from the façade to the pavement. It contains a pool, a planted strip and an area of coarse, green Andeer gravel that separates lime trees from the lavish ground floor window façade. The pool, which collects rainwater, forms the boundary of the front garden on the street side. The whole project was predicated on allowing surface water to evaporate or seep away on site,

Hofmannsthal, Hugo von: *"Lob des Gartens"* in: Killy, Walther (ed.): *Die Deutsche Literatur. Texte und Zeugnisse.* Vol 7. Munich 1988; p.286

Kienast, Dieter: *"10 Thesen zur Landschaftsarchitektur"* (1989) in: Professur für Landschaftsarchitektur ETH Zürich (ed.): *Dieter Kienast – Die Poetik des Gartens. Über Chaos und Ordnung in der Landschaftsarchitektur.* Basel Berlin Boston 2002; p. 207

Mühlebachstrasse in Zurich: The small but elegant screen of trimmed limes on the left-hand side of the street signals an unusual design idea.

The pool by the pavement; rainwater reservoir and urban design element in one.

Totally irresistible to children: accessible water in public space.

in other words to take it back into the natural cycle, rather than letting it disappear in the municipal sewerage system. The reservoir pool's precise surface extends along almost the full frontage of the building. Excess water from the roof is channelled first of all into the directly adjacent seepage strip, and only when this can no longer handle the quantity of water is it directed into the municipal drains.

An irregular row of densely planted limes, with their crowns severely trimmed to the height of the first cornice, form a dense shade of leaves that meets up with the roof of the entrance area. This means that the space is precisely formulated and conveys a new feeling of human scale. The leaf canopy is floodlit from below at night. As in a kit system, steel, water, stone and trees combine to form an abstract structure of urban nature that functions very well, but runs counter to any clichéd notions of a garden idyll. Passers-by, especially children, love this element of water in the street. At the same time the surface of the water registers every breath of wind that is felt in the city, reflects the sunlight into the treetops or into the interior of the adjacent offices. Unfortunately, this attractive element was not extended when the front garden area was enlarged recently.

Water in a whole variety of manifestations also plays a key part in the building's confined rear courtyard. The central office on the ground floor looks out over a kind of surrealistic stage, its centre accentuated by an immense concrete pot. This was derived from well typology, and is fed underground with roof water via a specially insulated piping system. When it rains heavily, the pot overflows and the water seeps away

into the surface of the courtyard – in principle, a huge seepage bed. The spatial boundary at the back of the small yard is formed by a light tufa wall, with water trickling down on to it from above. Moss and lichen are establishing themselves on the porous wall and gradually covering it with a greenish fur; it is worth paying this close attention. Fine grasses and cranesbill have rooted in the cracks and gaps in the tufa. These complement the lime-rich spring flora, which is interesting in terms of plant sociology. A vertical wet biotope is developing gradually and spontaneously within a strictly architectural framework, in the middle of the city. Until recently, a narrow bed of marsh iris separated the narrow water channel at the foot of the wall from the greenish gravel of the water-bound floor.

The simple concept of the spontaneously self-greening wet wall is formally reminiscent of Minimal Art by artists like Donald Judd, but conceptually also of the highly controversial fountain in Bern's Waisenhausplatz by the Surrealist artist Meret Oppenheim, who died in 1985. There a simple concrete column eight metres high had water trickling down it, transforming itself, since 1983, into an ecologically valuable "hanging garden." However, the image it presented offended mainstream notions of natural beauty. Here in Zurich, as in many other projects by Dieter Kienast, architectural form and natural processes combine in close symbiosis to create new gardens beyond traditional clichés. Nature in the city finds a new language.

Next two pages:
Seen from the conference room, the enormous well-head dominates the tiny courtyard.

The small porch at the building entrance and the trimmed canopy of the lime trees complement each other to form an ensemble.

The concrete wall on the left is overgrown
with wild vines, and on the right is the
spontaneously seeded calcareous tufa wall.
The well overflows after heavy rain.

Seen from above it becomes clear
how small the areaway for this Zurich
office building actually is.

The growth of moss, lichen and algae runs counter to the usual clichéd idea of nature in the city. The heavy carpet of plants detaches itself from time to time and the growth cycle starts again.

A park as a promise

Designers:
Zulauf, Seippel
and Schweingruber
landscape architects in
co-operation with
Hubacher und Härle
Architekten
Public park
Size: 1.75 hectares
Completed
in 1999 – 2001

Well-meaning commentators call the largest of the four new district parks in Oerlikon, Zurich "austere," but everybody who thinks a municipal park should offer picturesque groups of trees on a carpet of green grass finds the Oerliker Park hard to take: about 1,000 little trees, planted on just under two hectares of gravel without any greenery, placed in a strict grid pattern as if they were in a nursery, providing scarcely any shade. The design plans that the landscape architects Zulauf, Seippel und Schweingruber submitted to win the competition in 1996 showed "Living by the park" in a very different light: computer-generated images promised a green, shady hall of trees, of the kind familiar from Parisian town gardens or the magical Petersplatz in Basel. But people who lived by or used the park had hoped that this seductively designed promise would be redeemed rather more rapidly. And why not; ultimately a whole branch of the garden industry lives by selling images of nature off the shelf, "instant green," guaranteed to grow, and with the demand increasing as the landscape architects' computer simulations get more and more perfect.

But in reality the ideal garden and landscape image – to the extent that it ever comes about exactly as planned – cannot be created at the click of a mouse or subsequently preserved for ever, as nature's only enduring quality is that it is in a permanent state of change, always growing and transient. In a country whose product development and manufacturing perfectionism became world famous under the "Made in Switzerland" label, the landscape architect Rainer Zulauf feels increasingly threatened by ready-made images: "Unlike us landscape architects, architects often talk about finished mood images that can be opened out as if they were in a picture-book. They contain a certain range of colours, but they have nothing to say about change. […] I feel that I am greatly affect-

The sweet gum trees in the foreground and the ash trees in the background will gradually grow into a dense grove.

ed by finished images, by fixed images. The longer I live, the more clearly I see that the in-between is much more important."• The Oerliker Park is a controversial in-between situation: the continuous process should be central, not the finished product.

Zulauf, Rainer,
in an interview with
the author in
February 2002

Oerlikon, Zurich had been one of Switzerland's most important industrial centres since the mid-19th century. In the 1980s, it became involved in a profound structural change that saw the old machine-based industry disappearing. Since the nineties, a new district has started to emerge on an area of about 72 hectares on the northern outskirts of Zurich. It includes just under six hectares of open space that are excellently connected with the cultural landscape surrounding them. There were serious planning problems, only one of which was that the contaminated industrial land could not be reclaimed, but

A floor relief in coarse gravel with asphalt paths threading through it is a feature of a small section of the Oerliker Park.

had to be covered with asphalt, on which the Oerliker Park survives as if sitting on a tray. As well as this, it was not clear at the beginning of the project how quickly the new district would come into being and start to be filled with life. What if the new municipal park never became part of the city? Given these imponderables, Zulauf, Seippel and Schweingruber worked with the architects to develop a staggeringly simple project idea: young trees were to be planted in a grid pattern, and from this a dense volume of trees would gradually grow up, independent of the surrounding area, able to absorb a whole variety of uses, like a great, green hall.

Installing a hall of trees like this off the peg was not an option as it contradicted the emphasis on process for which the landscape architects stood. So instead of expensive fully-grown trees, 800 young

The timber-planked deck thrusts into the eastern, slightly lower half of the park.

A carpet of lawn spreads out under the trees in the eastern half of the park, in contrast with the western half.

Seen from the tower, the western half of the park with its timber deck and red folly still looks fairly bleak.

The red Park House in the centre of the park symbolizes common public use by the residents of the quarter.

Fresh green on a black water-bound surface – incomprehensible to many visitors to the park.

Individual structures, like the industrial chimney in the background, still provide reminders of former industrial use, while the new buildings, fountain, pavilion and tower, thrust into the foreground.

saplings, common ash from a whole variety of Swiss tree nurseries, and from Holland, Italy and Germany were planted, with 200 sweet gum trees, river birch, wild cherry and princess trees to provide a range of blossom highlights. Instead of the grass that so many people hankered after, there is a water-bound surface under most of the trees. So the specially developed wooden loungers and park benches look somewhat lost at the time of writing. This park is a promise. "It is like giving someone a bulb or a plant-pot with a hyacinth shoot in it," the landscape architect explains. "I am not forcing anyone to do without the finished product, but I am giving them something that can grow,

The ash trees have gained in green volume after only a few years, and are starting to establish the park's character.

that they can grow on. So I'm not depriving them of the finished picture, but offering them the experience of seeing the picture emerging." •

Ibid.

The striking concrete elements are embedded in the growing park like petrified organs: a red pavilion, a light green fountain table and a blue viewing tower 33 metres high. Similar to the bright red follies in the Parc de la Villette in Paris, dating from the early eighties, the red pavilion in Oerlikon on the edge of the extensive wooden deck offers various use options. Along with the 20-metre-long water-table, reminiscent of a classical Renaissance garden feature, it accentuates the importance of the clearing. As an area for action, it links the two park areas, which are separated by a residents' street. The tower serves as a look-out and vertical access element to the emergent tree-hall. Its steel spiral staircase is intended to make it possible to climb up through the leafy roof of the tree hall and look out over the roofs of Oerlikon to the surrounding urban and cultural landscape. The blue building functions as a fixed measure showing how the trees are growing, but as a piece of "memory of the tall chimneys in the former industrial quarter"• it has to compete with the authentic, elegant brick chimneys in sooty red that stood in the immediate vicinity until recently, as genuine evidence of industrial history.

The city of Zurich allowed itself to be convinced by the idea of the

"Neue Grünflächen für altes Industrie-quartier" in: Schweizer Baublatt no. 24, 24 March 2000; p. 5

The simple lighting elements still loom too large between the young ash trees. This imbalance will change only with time.

growing park, and the nearby residents, who moved into the new district much sooner than expected, will watch more or less patiently as the young ash trees, competing for light, grow taller and finally form a hall with narrow trunks almost without branches, their leafy roof spreading out like a green canopy. Forestry methods will be used to thin out the dense stand of trees gradually until the year 2025. Trees that die off early are not to be replaced for the sake of the dynamics of the space. These are the rules of the game. If one listens to the landscape architects carefully, one cannot help summoning up the image of the completed park, but "perhaps it won't happen," as Rainer Zulauf remarks, and what then? "The Oerliker Park is one of four such features, just part of a jigsaw puzzle offering a special kind of experience": • an open-ended natural process.

Zulauf, Rainer, in an interview with the author in February 2002

This park is still not complete, and perhaps it never will be – and there is a principle behind this.

The red pavilion harmonizes with its surroundings in front of the new, red-rendered homes on the southern edge of the park.

Green fur on a steel skeleton

Herzog, Jacques
quoted from: ARCH+
142, July 1998; p. 34

"I can imagine that we have reached a point at which dealing with nature and integrating landscape into urban development can no longer be avoided. Any architectural intervention always entails working with nature: destruction and repair. Landscape and garden architecture are going to grow explosively." • The Basel architect Jacques Herzog prophesied this a few years ago. Since then many architects have used words like "landscaping," "inversion," "decontextualization" or "hybridization" in their search for successful symbiosis between landscape and city, garden and house, plant and building – with or without the help of landscape architects.

The gigantic 100-metre-long, 34-metre-wide and 17-metre-high "green opera house" in the Zurich suburb of Oerlikon is one such attempt to create a hybrid structure using nature and architecture in the newly emerging district of Zurich North. When the competition was announced in 1997 the responsible department, Grün Stadt Zürich, was seeking landscape design ideas for the MFO park, named after the Oerlikon Machine Factory. As one of four new district parks it was intended to create usable open and recreational space on the former industrial site, which was to become a densely developed residential and working area. The responsible architects at Burckhardt + Partner, Heinz Moser and Roger Nussbaumer, however, felt that for urban development reasons a green open space was not needed here, but a built volume to intensify the urban quality of the location. The concept of a park-house as the "largest garden arbour in the world," as the architects' information flyer put it, suggested itself forcibly as a solution to this conflict of aims.

The landscape architects responsible for the nearby Oerliker Park deliberately did not set out to create a finished green solution, but trusted instead that years of natural growth would turn a densely planted field of trees into an impressively voluminous, green tree-hall, similar to the one in the Jardin du Luxembourg in Paris. In contrast to this, Burckhardt + Partner used tried-and-tested architectural resources to achieve their desired aim more quickly. They employed sophisticated technology to place 290,000 kilograms of steel, 32 kilometres of steel cables and wire, and 870 square metres of wooden and metal grids to place a massive framework in the open space. It looks like a piece of furniture on an artificially raised area of the slightly sloping plot.

The steel skeleton is also supposed to be a reminder of the lost industrial identity of the district. Like a larger-than-life climbing frame, it offers some amazing spatial experiences. The theatrical nature of the structure, reminiscent of warehouse halls, is most in evidence at night,

Designers:
Burckhardt + Partner
architects in co-operation
with Raderschall
landscape architects
Public park
Size: 8,500 m²
Completed in
2001 – 2002

A rich variety of different climbing species are slowly growing up cables from the bottom of the great steel framework.

Balcony-like stands tower up inside the "biggest arbour in the world," providing both viewpoints and performance places.

Flights of steps compensate for the height difference on the site and create an even base for the building.

Simple urban furniture on a carpet of green recycling glass: wooden benches, a round pool and column-like pipe-vines.

when the transparent interior with its neon tubes and bright spots is bathed in pale green light. The impression of a stage is reinforced by the viewing platforms that thrust into the hall like balconies, but most particularly by a rectangular field in the rear part of the hall, which is slightly sunken and covered with green glass chippings. With its decorative seating in the style of wooden loungers and a small, circular water trough, this field looks like the absurd, meaningless hotel lobby from a play by Samuel Beckett in the harsh light of the spots.

From a height of 17 metres you look down from the timber-planked viewing deck on the roof of the "green opera house" into the green lobby and wait for the first visitors to become unwitting actors on the absurd set and start to present themselves. The spectators on the roof of the hall enjoy the feeling that they are on the deck of a container ship stranded in the city, and look for striking landmarks in the immediate vicinity. This lofty, airy timber deck is already one of the most popular meeting places for young people in the area, and a lot of people are fascinated by the goose-pimply feeling they get when looking down into the depths through the brightly lit grid, while others are already working out the first tests for their courage on the easily accessible steel structure.

And nature? Apart from a good dozen narrow hedges connecting the indoor and outdoor spaces at ground level, 1,200 creepers and climbers of 100 different species are to proliferate to the full height of the steel cable-covered outer façade of the "green opera house" over the next few years, covering the gigantic building on its little feet with thick green fur. An ingenious irrigation system and a battery of plant troughs on the top floor are there to ensure that nature, given the inventors' ambitious vision and the hard conditions in the lofty heights, does not simply give up the ghost and that the green camouflage does not ultimately start sporting holes.

The city of Zurich's courage and willingness to experiment in its search for up-to-date expressive forms in landscape architecture have been impressive in recent years, and are needed in the future; expressive urban open spaces – preferably well constructed and not distorted – will be luxuries in the cities of tomorrow.

The project has in fact already won some prizes, including the Public Design Prize in 2003, and in the same year it was given an honourable mention when the German Landscape Architecture Prize was awarded, but it is in fact not yet complete. It will not be possible to continue by building a planted, 17-metre-high forest of poles until an office building is demolished at the southern, open end of the hall. The yellowish façade of the old building still provides the one missing interior

Visitors to the platform with a view towards the Zürichberg feel as though they are on the deck of a container ship stranded in the town.

A gallery with large plant troughs in the airy heights ensures that the green fur will cover the roof of the steel skeleton as well.

An ingenious irrigation and cultivation system is required to transform the 17 metre high space grid into a "green opera-house."

wall of the "opera house" and looks like a consistent, disturbingly authentic continuation of the extensive flooring inside the hall, which is also yellowish and made of water-bound lime marl. But soon this building will come down as well, and it will be very interesting to see what new structure – planted or not planted –, reminiscent of the old one, will emerge in its place.

In future the spaces between the inside and outside walls will be experienced as shady tunnels.

Dark green yew hedges link the glass carpet of the lobby with the outside of the building.

The creeper-covered steel cable constructions link the greenish glass carpet on the floor with the roof like slender green funnels.

A *sunken* hortus conclusus

Landscape architects:
Agence Ter,
with Domino architects
Garden in a private
foundation
Size: approx. 1,300 m²
Completed in 1993

Every garden represents our desired ideal of the Garden of Eden to a certain extent. The more man felt helplessly at the mercy of the powers of nature, the more he cut himself off, withdrawing behind the protective walls of his earthly paradise. Cultivated, benign nature developed both in the oasis gardens of the Egyptian god-kings and in the medieval *hortus conclusus*. Water, the source of life, was central to the shady splendour of trees and flowers, in the form of a pool or fountain.

Anyone standing outside the south entrance to the Fondation Louis Jeantet de Médicine on the busy Route de Florissant in Geneva would not immediately imagine that there is a garden behind the massive

concrete wall. It is only when looking through the narrow window in the stainless steel gate that you first get a sense of the sunken oasis garden. And if you are allowed to pass through the fortified sliding door, a slate-covered walkway will take you two metres down to a little square patio surrounded by walls four and a half metres high. The gate shuts again, preventing the outside world from intruding. A monastery garden?

The courtyard occupies an area of 15 by 15 metres and is filled with the sound of softly splashing water. It is paced with rectangular black state slabs, with rich green moss growing between them. The fluent, ordered structure of the slate slabs is remin-

The street front of the *hortus conclusus* on the Route de Florissant in Geneva seems uninviting at a first glance.

A ramp leads down to the garden of the Fondation Jeantet.

142

iscent of rafted tree-trunks driven together at a dam by river currents. The ground seems to flow; the only places where movement stops are points at which the client added slabs for functional reasons. The carpet of moss between the slabs reinforces the impression of a cool water-garden in the middle of the city's heat. A water-channel one metre wide runs all round. Like a shadow-joint, it separates the steel-edged paving from the concrete walls. Water flows glitteringly into the channel from the apertures that are let into the walls at regular intervals. Little scarlet cherry trees spread out the upright funnel of their branches, unfolding their summer-green shady canopy at a height of about four metres. In April, when the cherry trees are showing their lavish pink blossom, visitors feel as though they are entering a Japanese meditation garden. In autumn, the orange to scarlet foliage contrasts with the grey of the plain exposed concrete.

The fact that there is no seating in the patio suggests that the garden was not planned as a place to spend time in. On the contrary, it is a linking and reception space for a new, underground auditorium in the neighbouring residential building, that is reached through a swing door from the patio, at the same level. Like the auditorium, the garden was the result of an architecture competition announced by the Fondation Jeantet in 1993 with the aim of developing concepts for converting the Villa Edelstein for use as a new building by the foundation. The Geneva architectural practice Domino won the competition and joined up with the Paris landscape architecture practice Agence Ter, Henri Bava, Michel Hoessler and Olivier Philippe for the design of the outdoor areas. As the villa would scarcely be able to hold its own in the urban context against the tall blocks of flats in the surrounding area, and only a little remained of the original garden, the architectural team decided to surround the building, which is in the Italian Neo-Renaissance style, with a large monolithic pedestal, indeed to place it on this pedestal, which takes up the whole of the plot. Only a fringe of existing and newly planted trees and a narrow

The old Villa Edelstein sits proudly above the canopy of leaves.

bed of bamboo screen the terrace off, to some extent, from the adjacent housing.

The substructure is not just the new plane of reference on which the villa confidently presents itself. It also takes over the function of the boundary terrace, thrusting out like a drawer from site, which slopes downwards by about two and a half metres, and pointing to the new auditorium. Originally all surfaces of the concrete pedestal were to be covered with black slate. In the end, exposed concrete was chosen for the sidewalls for reasons of cost; slate was used only for paving purposes. The topography makes it impossible to look into the inside of the plot and into the garden from the Route de Florissant.

The landscape architects' aim was not to use the garden as green decoration but as a central component of the new constellation of buildings. Hence the patio was punched out of the pedestal. Its negative volume relates directly to the proportions of the villa: its ground plan adopts the external dimensions of the foundation building. When entering the villa from the terrace, one feels like standing on a raised stage in the middle of the city. Seen from here, the garden seems like a minimalist installation, a piece of abstract marquetry on the stage floor. It is fringed by two U-shaped pools set at ground level. They reflect the sky, and make the edge of the patio into an expressive feature. The greenish-black floor covering shimmers through the semi-transparent veil of the treetops.

Rich green moss grows between the dark slate slabs.

The initial plan was to make the pools into large-volume water reservoirs, four and a half metres deep and one metre wide. The water would have flowed into the courtyard through their perforated inner walls. But this expensive concept was then abandoned, and pools one and a half metres deep were constructed instead, with the water likewise flowing into the sunken garden through slits. Two very narrow

The water splashes out of narrow slits in the sidewalls into a narrow moat.

A moat provides the border for the inner edge of the garden courtyard, which is sunk by 4.5 metres.

Narrow stairs lead out on to the patio.

From the ground-level entrance to the old villa there is scarcely a hint that the sunken garden exists.

flight of steps lead down into the garden at the point where the pools intersect. The landscape architect Henri Bava was inspired to create these striking stairways by the embankment steps on the Ile de la Cité in Paris. His aim was that only one person at a time should be able to use the steps and come down into the garden, and in fact the steps are just wide enough for one person to descend. The steps are accompanied by two narrow water-channels clad with structured stainless steel to create a lively, glittering pattern in the flowing water – a motif that is also familiar from the *chadars*, the cascades in Indian Mogul gardens.

At night, when the trees and walls are lit from below and illuminate the water, it is like plunging into a mysterious, silent underwater world. This contemporary urban variation on the *hortus conclusus* proves that the paradise garden has lost nothing of its original force as an archetype.

Joints in panoramic view

It would have been difficult to make the philosophy professor and garden theoretician Christian Cay Lorenz Hirschfeld from Kiel on Germany's Baltic coast summon up any enthusiasm for the Alpine mountain world. "If nature has shaped one land that combines most excellently delightful views with an astonishing scope and variety of heroic objects, then that country is Switzerland," wrote the author of Theorie der Gartenkunst in 1779, yet: "I am not speaking of the wild areas where nature has accumulated nothing but her frights and terrors, but of the mild areas that are distinguished by a collection of all landscape charms that are either far from the sight of those terrible mountains, or where they only raise their shimmering summits in the distance and see a certain solemn majesty spreading from the most extreme horizon."•

Hirschfeld, Christian Cay Lorenz: *Theorie der Gartenkunst.* Volume One. Leipzig 1779; p. 33

Hirschfeld did not suspect that barely 50 years after the publication of his reflections, which became a standard work, a romantic enthusiasm for the natural sublime would drive people into the mountains in hordes and would set the rapid development of Alpine tourism in motion. This onslaught did not just damage the character of the landscape in many places, it also impacted on people's sensitivity to the different qualities of nature that Hirschfeld is invoking here.

The Ticino landscape architect Paolo Bürgi, working on an unusual landscape project on the Cardada near Locarno, is pursing the ambitious goal of sharpening up our somewhat jaded perceptions in this respect. The project was triggered by the establishment of a cable car service from Orselina to the Cardada. The first cableway on this route came into service as early as 1952. After the transport capacity had been raised several times, a decision was taken in 1996 to renew the system completely; the Ticino architect Mario Botta was commissioned with this major project. The new cableway was officially opened in June 2000, and has been carrying people to a height of 1,340 metres even more efficiently since then. Here visitors are not only offered the usual programme of winter sports, food and drink, walking and hiking. Paolo Bürgi wondered how he could address and enhance the visitors' sensibilities without simply providing additional attractions. He created an ensemble consisting of a play footpath, a viewing walkway, a geological information station and a musical wood.

When leaving the mountain station with its futuristic architectural language you unexpectedly step on to an austerely designed carpet of granite. Large-format slabs, a traditional building material in Ticino gardens, have been laid in a precise fishbone pattern here, with the

Landscape architect:
Paolo Bürgi
Public landscape
intervention
Completed in
1996–2000

Floating above the trees of Orselina the cableway rides up to the Cardada at 1,340 metres.

The viewing walkway leads to the light through the tops of the spruce trees.

The path through the treetops promises wonderful views of the Ticino mountain landscape.

grassed joints becoming wider and wider towards the edge of the slope. Bürgi had a simple fountain cut out of a tree trunk. Its angular basic form is a response to the strict simplicity of the floor covering. This attractive carpet concludes in a long, wide wooden bench whose basic form is just as geometrical as that of the slab covering. Its angles indicate the point where the path divides. It leads down on the left to the Promontorio paesaggistico and up on the right to the Osservatorio geologico.

After a few hundred metres the path to the Promontorio paesaggistico broadens into a geometrically shaped square. This forms a visual abutment to a very long, narrow viewing walkway made of steel that thrusts up through the dark tops of the spruce trees. The path leads into the light on granite slabs. Little signs in the paving accompany visitors under the elegant pylons until they reach the funnel-like opening of the walkway: the view over Lago Maggiore is overwhelming.

Small explanatory tablets on the railing of the viewing walkway explain the mysterious symbols that one is confronted with along the way: they tell us about the origins of life. Anyone who finds that too didactic can simply enjoy the breathtaking view or hear the children's laughter as they enjoy themselves on the distant play path. This crosses the wooded slope below the walkway and is equipped with all sorts of play apparatus intended to stimulate children in a landscape that could hardly be more stimulating.

Visitors leaving the walkway and completing the energetic climb to the summit of the Cimetta arrive at the geological observatory at a height of 1,670 metres. This is probably the most interesting of Bürgi's landscape interventions. He has inserted a large circular platform with bands of rock eating into it at the sides. The rock is made to stand out

from its surroundings by this simple intervention and looks sculptural: bizarre finds, presented on a plate without edge.

The surface of the platform is divided into two different levels of lightness by a covering of fine, grey sand. Polished stone samples are displayed on both segments of the circle, differing in their number and colouring. The segments of the circle are separated by a red line: this symbolizes the Insubric line, also known as the Periadriatic fault, the great southern valley running the length of the Alps, a kind of geological joint that opened up between the central and the southern Alps about 200 million years ago. This is where the different rocks shown as samples on the observation platform meet.

Even at this place, which has a meditative quality because of its archaic and at the same time abstract form, visitors are not left alone with their thoughts, but instructed. Here too there are small information panels on the platform railings, providing geological information, revealing something that is invisible to the layman: effectively the building plan for this grandiose landscape, formed on timescales – and

Pylon and tree, architecture and nature in an elegant dialogue.

Paolo Bürgi's Osservatorio geologico is at a height of 1,670 metres.

Looming rock seems to eat into the immaculate surface of the circular viewing platform.

Sometimes the view from the platform is lost in the clouds.

The Ginkgo leaf as symbol of dimensions that are important for the history of the earth but concealed in the landscape for the lay eye.

Nature untreated and treated: the natural colours of the stone are revealed only when it is cut and polished.

A red line running across the platform marks the Insubric line, the "joint" between the central and the southern Alps.

still being formed – that are not visible to the tourist eye. Bürgi uses the traditional form of the Alpine panorama and combines a look into the geological depths with the sweeping view of the landscape, the scientific and rational explorer's eye with the romantic and sentimental enjoyment of nature. Both views, sometimes self-contradictory, have determined man's relationship with nature for about 200 years.

View from the Osservatorio geologico down to Lago Maggiore with its little islands in the mist.

Landscape in abstract folds

Landscape architects:
Kienast Vogt Partner
Public park
Size: approx. 5 hectares
Created for the Graz
International
Horticultural Show
2000

The scenery is surreal: like sleepwalkers the public move through a landscaped stage set with grassy pyramids rising to a height of up to eight metres. Spectators become protagonists, disappearing between geometrically shaped folds in the earth, exploring terraced pyramids or enjoying the shade under small groups of trees, so that they can also look out over the moving second version of the abstract scenery on the surface of the woodland pool. All this is overlaid with a sound carpet typical of the late 20th century: the chatting of visitors, occasionally the howling jets of a plane taking off and heavenly music. "[…] you bring us a completely new landscape, you create a sense of space that I have never felt before in the open air. You prove that given an ingenious mind and precise use of the craft, it is not absolutely necessary to use this valuable material soil in a way as the forces of nature do. You do not create an imitation of a natural event, but you create a work in a way that we abstract painters and sculptors have been trying to achieve by concrete means for years."• This letter from Hans Fischli, the author of this enthusiastic account, could have been aimed at the

Fischli, Hans:
Letter to Ernst
Cramer dated 26
August 1959; Archiv
für Schweizer
Landschaftsarchi-
tecktur, Rapperswil,
dossier 01.03.013
English translation
from: Weilacher,
Udo: *Visionary
Gardens. Modern
Landscapes by Ernst
Cramer.* Basel Berlin
Boston 2001; p. 115

landscape architect of the "Berggarten" at the 2000 International Horticultural Show in Graz. But in fact the distinguished architect, painter, sculptor and then director of the Kunstgewerbeschule and Kunstgewerbemuseum in Zurich was writing a tribute in 1959 to a brilliant work by the visionary garden architect Ernst Cramer at the First Swiss Horticultural Exhibition on the shores of Lake Zurich.

The temporary Poet's Garden at the G|59 show in Zurich, an abstract composition made up of four grassy pyramids, a terraced cone and a right-angled expanse of water with an iron sculpture by Bernhard Luginbühl can be seen as the precursor of Kienast Vogt Partner's mountain garden. Ernst Cramer, also

The abstract pattern of folds in the Graz Mountain Garden can be made out clearly from the viewing tower.

from Zurich, was familiar with the cultural and garden-historical models for his earthworks, the ancient Egyptian pyramids and tumuli by Prince Hermann Pückler-Muskau. While the Pückler pyramids were still very close to the ancient Egyptian tomb structures in form and function, Cramer's garden consisted of pyramids with three unequal sides. They were intended as artistic structures without any specific purpose, as Cramer was primarily interested in developing a modern landscape design language. His radical work was honoured by the Museum of Modern Art in New York as a pioneering achievement of modern garden architecture in 1964.•

Cf. Kassler,
Elizabeth B.:
*Modern gardens
and the landscape.*
New York 1964

Dieter Kienast greatly admired these modern landscapes and consistently further developed Cramer's radical design approach. 40 years after the 1959 show, Kienast was also able to benefit from his knowl-

edge of Land Art, which had caused a sensation with spectacular earthworks in American deserts from the late sixties onwards. While Cramer's earthworks were still free-standing individual structures, in Graz 29,000 cubic metres of soil were used to create an earth sculpture that people could walk on. This *hortus conclusus* was framed by a steep grassy rampart about five metres high like a monastery wall, which had two striking openings cut into it with runs of exposed concrete. Between the 26 large earth formations, which are accessed by a network of geometrically cut paths, are remains of a monotonous spruce plantation that was already on the site. Rather than stripping out these ecologically inferior trees, clearings were created and the trees headed down. Seen through the shady filter of the slender spruce trunks the sunny slopes of the earth pyramids make a particularly pleasing impression. Large individual trees, some newly planted, many found on site, are natural extras on scene in the northern area of the garden, accentuating the various spatial sequences there. The dialogue between the basic architectural concept and the natural quality that has become a distinguishing stylistic trait of Kienast Vogt Partner's projects, also occurs at the centrally placed woodland pool. Its basic form is geometrical and it acts as a reflecting pool and habitat, complementing the composition of art and nature. Two pyramids whose stepped sides were intended as a grandstand for visitors offer a view over the futuristically staged landscape.

Particularly attractive spatial sequences appear between the earth pyramids.

To satisfy the garden visitors' desire for fragrance and colour, and to avoid monotony in the lawns, the landscape architects planted individual sides of the pyramids uniformly with different shrubs and perennials with decorative blossom and leaves. Scilla, lavender, lady's mantle, ivy and dwarf bamboo, some planted in patterns, are intended to provide a range of blossom and foliage effects all the year round. Elsewhere, large, quarry-rough limestone blocks created a large, slightly sloping area of almost 1,000 square metres on which a large number of plants enjoying dryness and warmth have found their ideal location – a contemporary interpretation of the traditional Alpine garden. Dieter Kienast was quite sure that austerity alone can be very

Visitors explore the unusual scenery.

The little tree seems to part the earth masses effortlessly: graphic plant patterns emphasize the artificiality of the Mountain Garden.

dogmatic in garden design, thus loving the interplay between formal architectural order and the natural dynamics of the vegetation's growth and flowering. But instead of indiscriminately plundering the traditional garden design repertoire of Baroque and landscape gardens, he wanted to develop an independent design language for the 21st century, firmly anchored in the garden and also in garden culture. Unlike the temporary Poet's Garden, which the garden designers' community of the fifties saw as mere provocation, the "Berggarten" was retained as a public park once the exhibition was over. Its precision means that it needs to be tended as carefully and expertly as many a historical masterpiece. In a polemic against the widespread design loquacity of horticultural shows, Dieter Kienast expressed a wish for "everyday, intellectual, sensual, atmospheric, green and colourful, large and small, light and dark, open and closed, ordered and wild gardens, full of poetry." • He has made his own wish come true in Graz.

Kienast, Dieter:
*"Zwischen Poesie und
Geschwätzigkeit"*
from: Garten und
Landschaft 1/1994;
p. 17

The strips of lavender in the foreground are not yet in bloom, but aromatic fragrance will soon accompany the surreal scene.

Large quarry-rough limestone blocks create an Alpine garden of almost 1,000 square metres in which plants loving dryness and warmth flourish.

Terraced pyramids act as seating by the woodland pool.

The blossoming strips of lady's mantle place glowing accents in front of the dark woodland setting.

The landscape runs down between the dark spruce stands towards the pool in elegant folds.

Reflections in the woodland lake of the
earthworks enhance the experience
of landscape art.

The abstract landscape stage set gives
impetus to artistic presentations.

The garden is enclosed by a rampart
five metres high.

Nature fragments in a geometrical network

Landscape architect:
Bet Figueras,
with architect
Carlos Ferrater
Botanical Gardens
Size: 15 hectares
Completed in 1999

Botanical gardens came into being long before botany developed as a discipline in its own right in the 18th and 19th centuries. In fact, they emerged through university researchers' scientific interest in medicinal plants and their healing properties. The formal aesthetic of the 16th-century horti medici ground plans was reminiscent of monastic gardens for herbs and medicinal plants, and the criteria by which they were divided up were not merely functional. Their clear geometrical structure reflects ideal worldviews mainly derived from classical antiquity. The Botanical Garden in Padua, created in 1545, is one of the first of its kind and was used as a model for many others in Europe. Its circular, hierarchical ground plan, with a precisely square, four-part bed inscribed in it, symbolized all nature coming together microcosmically under the ordering rule of man in the age of the Renaissance. Society's relationship with nature has changed fundamentally in past centuries, along with our formerly closed picture of the world. This also affects the appearance of the few new botanical gardens that are created today. The Jardí Botànic in Barcelona, completed in 1999, lies on the southern slope of the Montjuïc with magnificent views of the Catalan capital. Like its predecessors, it is primarily intended for scientific investigation of the nature of the plant world – Mediterranean in this case. But its design, developed by the landscape architect Bet Figueras in co-operation with the architect Carlos Ferrater, unmistakably speaks the language of the early 21st century, characterized by complex, irregular geometries in the allocation of space and an unreserved use of large exposed concrete and raw steel elements for paths and walls in the landscape.

Already on the wide concrete path, structured by a complex pattern of joints, leading to the entrance of the Botanical Gardens, you are passing figuratively through the eight landscape zones around the globe

The concrete paths zigzag down the slope to Carlos Ferrater's entrance building.

Existing vegetation, like the large umbrella pine in the background, was of course integrated into the new Botanical Garden.

Forms, colours and structures, natural or artificial, set each other off well.

with similar Mediterranean-style climates with long, dry summer months and mild, rainy winters. Walking in the shade of umbrella pines, the visitor crosses the Catalan words for Australia, California, Chile, South Africa and for the Mediterranean regions of the Canary Islands, the east Mediterranean, North Africa and the Iberian Peninsula, the letters set in the ground in large steel characters. The Botanical Gardens are dedicated to researching, protecting and presenting typical plant communities from these zones.

Once you have passed through the large steel entrance with the JBB inscription and left behind the low entrance building, which blends in with the topography, an impressive view opens up over the geometrically shaped lake and on to the freshly planted slope. This builds up in front of the visitor like a terraced landscape, with many paths, triangular, jagged retaining walls in rust-red Corten steel, and light grey exposed concrete. The designers were clearly determined to conserve

Next two pages: A wooden walkway crosses the lake and leads straight into the depths of the gardens.

The beauty of the Mediterranean plants makes a particular impact within the strict framework of the landscape design.

The intricately structured foliage of the Peruvian pepper and the rigid leaves of the hemp palm flank the two sides of the path.

The place will soon look like an oasis between the great palm trees in the Spanish heat.

the slope with the walls as an abstract reminder of the artificially terraced culture landscapes of the Mediterranean, now under threat.

The unusual division of the whole site into triangular areas planted in different ways is a result of the basic concept of stretching a network of triangles over the topography of the place. Rather like trigonometrical survey networks, this adapts flexibly to the terrain, producing an innovative, hybrid-looking landscape with an artificial, computer-generated grid structure that has fragments of nature woven into it. The extensive network of wide concrete paths essentially illustrates this network of triangles in the terrain, at the same time guaranteeing comfortable access, complemented by short, steep flights of steps. Specially designed seating in folded steel is not exactly comfortable to sit on, but underlines the unusual styling of the gardens.

A long wooden walkway over the large, expressively shaped pool makes an atmospheric start to the tour of the various Mediterranean vegetation zones. On the slope side, acute-angled steel walls thrust into the water, which, like a mirror, provides an optical double for the adjacent landscape with its striking North African date palms. The fresh green rushes and typhaceae stand out particularly attractively against the rust-red surface of the Corten steel. The path then leads out of the dip in the terrain and up the slope, from which the view opens up more and more over the Olympic sports facilities and the surrounding countryside to the sea on the south side, the Llobregat estuary and the mountain ranges on the horizon. High above the lively Mediterranean city of Barcelona, the Botanical Gardens are a peaceful and relaxing place.

With the hurly-burly of the city at its feet, the garden becomes a refuge for people seeking peace and quiet.

The plants and shrubs have still developed only sparsely in many areas, and so the paths seem somewhat oversize. But this will change with the passage of time as the vegetation grows. Visitors are given a sense of how plant communities change with time. It is already a special experience to wander through the various pictures the vegetation provides, accompanied by aromatic fragrances and the shrieks of green parrots, flocking to devour the first garden fruits.

A young classic with two faces

Landscape architects:
Dani Freixes and
Vincente Miranda
Public park
Size: approx. 2.7 hectares
Completed in
1985–1986

The little municipal Parc del Clot, set in the middle of a densely developed sixties and seventies residential and commercial quarter, can be called a classic of late 20th-century landscape architecture even though is has been in existence for barely 20 years. Current and historical structures are superimposed in a complex pattern and create new images. It is not entirely clear whether it is actually a park or a square. But perhaps it is precisely this ambiguity that has recently put it in the centre of discussion about the future design of municipal parks.

With its eye on the 1992 Olympic Games, Barcelona invested a great deal of energy and creativity in the mid-eighties in a programme of parks, squares and other public facilities for the benefit of the city's residents and to attract tourists. In the first place it was the careful treatment of inner-city public spaces, the striking architectural design of parks and squares and the intelligent integration of fine art into public space that were seen as exemplary and allowed the Catalan metropolis to become an internationally acknowledged model for the design of inner-city open spaces.

One of the most important strategies for creating new open spaces, which also became a model for other European cities, was based on a requirement in the 1976 general plan for Barcelona. This stated that former industrial land should be placed at the disposal of the public. The closure of old slaughterhouses, factories, workshops and quarries or railway facilities released space that could be transformed into parks and squares in the densely developed city. Often parts of the old industrial plant were included in the design and used to accommodate partly public institutions like libraries, for example.

The hard core of the park, inventively reinterpreted industrial ruins, overgrown with ivy.

The Parc del Clot was created in 1985 and 1986, to plans by the architects Dani Freixes and Vicente Miranda on land formerly occupied by railway workshops belonging to the Red Nacional de los Ferrocarriles Españoles (Renfe). Renfe had used this 27,000 square metre site until the mid-20th century; it was originally on the edge of a village northeast of the city that was caught up by ultra-rapid urban expansion in the course of time.

The surviving façades and an imposing chimney-stack that still enclose the northern half of the park – like romantic ruins in a classical landscaped park – are reminiscent of the former factory setting with its industrial halls and chimneys in red brick. The chimney stack, which is visible from some distance, marks the north-eastern corner of the park, where steep steps climb up from the lower urban quarter through the old factory archway into the park. A raised walkway and a long pergola section lead diagonally from the opposite sides of the park and from the adjacent residential area to the chimney, crossing the two differently characterized halves of the site: the northern section is designed like a park, and the southern half conceived like a square.

The northern section, accentuated by a large, naturalistically shaped grassy mound, is to be read as a landscape quotation. Its flanks are covered with magnificent Mediterranean blossom, while the foot of the slope is enclosed on three sides by a kind of small woodland belt, a dense stand of umbrella pines.

Hidden behind the woodland fringe, in the northern corner of the park, is part of the skeleton of the old factory hall vault. Liberated from the roof, it looks like an ancient pavilion. In the shady centre of this ivy-clad structure, in the middle of a square reflecting pool, the large, expressive bronze sculpture "Rites of Spring" by the American artist Bryan Hunt creates a meditative mood. Only the whoops of children

A wide flight of steps, flanked by this district park's most famous landmark, the factory chimney, leads up into the landscaped section.

The landscaped hill in the park provides a view of the roofs in the adjacent residential quarter.

The "Rites of Spring" sculpture accentuates the centre of a shady Mediterranean garden, formerly a factory hall belonging to Renfe, the Spanish railway system.

The border between the park section and the square section, crossed by a pedestrian bridge.

Compelling axial pathways structure the park and help people to find their bearings.

playing happily in the nearby playground, which is also framed with
umbrella pines, penetrate this meditative space.

At the eastern foot of the hill, which owes its existence to shifted
building rubble, a small expanse of water with a stylized beach defines
the scene. Rather like a little aqueduct, the old brick façade with its
segmented-arch windows thrusts between the hill and the adjacent,
tree-flanked street. In fact water does run along the top of the wall; it
pours into the pool as a water-curtain 25 metres wide, providing a
refreshing sound backdrop and noticeable cooling in the intense heat.
The architecturally designed southern half of the park presents a formal contrast with the varied miniature landscape; it consists of a
square at a lower level, framed by two large flights of steps for sitting
on. This area became three metres lower after the factory hall had
been demolished to basement level. The steps, but above all the pergola walkway that crosses above the square, provide comfortable
places for watching the young people enjoying themselves in the
square. Four large columns of lights ensure that their tireless ball
games do not have to come to an end, even long after night has fall-
en. Carefully directed illumination hightlights the landscape and
architectural backdrops all over the Parc del Clot.

The park was very popular with nearby residents from the outset.

The old brick façade of the industrial
architecture with its segmental arches
borders the park to the north and
is sometimes closed off with a curtain
of water.

The young people's games can be watched from the edge of the sunken square as if from a grandstand.

They like the different ways the parkland and the square can be used, with a niche for almost every age group. But the striking composition of the images, especially in the park section linked with romantic impressions from English landscape gardens, is another reason why people are so fascinated by "their" park. Picturesque ruins, set in an Arcadian ambience, were a popular motif even in the 18th century.

This park rose to be a much-quoted model in the field of international landscape architecture, precisely because of its inventive treatment of the industrial remains found there, and the successful reinterpretation and re-use of the factory ruins. Multi-optional 21st-century society likes its hybrid character, which promises two things: an ideal image of beautiful nature as a quotation of "landscape" in the city and also the quotation of the "square" concept, offering high-quality, culturally rich urban life.

In the garden of the fateful cards

Designer:
Niki de Saint-Phalle
Private park
Size: approx. 1.6 hectares
Completed in
1979 – 1998

She was just 25 years old, a model and an angry young woman coming from a good family who, as she later confessed, might well have been locked up for ever in a lunatic asylum in darker times because of her psychological instability. At that time, in 1955, she came across a masterpiece of garden architecture that moved her deeply: the Parc Güell, created by the Catalan architect Antoni Gaudí in Barcelona. Faced with the inspired expressiveness that the naturalistic formal language, the colourful mosaics and lush Mediterranean vegetation of Gaudí's work – started around 1900 – still emanates today, she was fired with an uncontrollable desire to create her own paradise garden one day. "Twenty-four years later I would embark on the biggest adventure of my life, the Tarot Garden." • Anyone visiting the former quarry near Garavicchio in Tuscany today finds the vital expressive quality of the place irresistible, and senses the powerful presence of Niki de Saint-Phalle, who worked in her paradise garden for over a decade from 1979, and even lived there for certain periods, until she finally died in 2002 of the late consequences of her excessive artistic work with polyester, a material that is damaging to health.

de Saint-Phalle, Niki:
The Tarot Garden.
Lausanne 1999;
p. 2

Always interested in the metaphysical aspects of life, Niki de Saint-Phalle chose the 22 images of the Great Arcana as Leitmotiv for the most important work of her life. These Tarot trump cards have been used in esoteric circles since the early 20th century as a source of self-knowledge and for fortune-telling, and they have also fascinated a large number of artistic personalities since then. The figures of the Great Arcana are symbolic in nature and represent basic archetypal characters. Thus for example the Fool stands for the archetype of the child or the pure fool, who approaches life naïvely but openly and without prejudice, all innocence and purity; while the Emperor embodies the archetype of the father, standing for the power of the rational spirit over chaotic nature. Niki de Saint-Phalle transformed the 22 fateful cards into extremely expressive, colourful sculptures in different sizes and degrees of complexity, fitting them self-confidently in the Macchia, the hilly landscape of the Garrigue. With the exception of topographical interventions, laying out a tangle of pathways and creating related sightlines, the artist was not mainly concerned with garden design measures. She was primarily interested in creating a sculpture garden. Hence Mediterranean spontaneous vegetation, the "natural" and "untouched" setting, provides the more or less neutral ground on which the figures are placed.

Similarly to the open Tarot rules, routes between the sculptures among the holm oaks, downy oaks, olive trees and many Mediterranean shrubs

Cheerfully glittering figures greet visitors on the plain from the green hills of the coastal range, enticing them into the Tarot Garden.

can be chosen as wished, so the pathway of fate in the figurative sense is neither fixed unambiguously nor necessarily predictable. And yet it is possible to detect points of emphasis where several large sculptures come together to form impressive ensembles or where Niki de Saint-Phalle and her numerous helpers have made certain cards, the Emperor, for example, into a real structural complex. The garden has been officially open to the public since 1998. Mysterious points of colourful reflected light entice visitors on the coastal plain into the wooded hills from a distance, into a world full of complex levels of meaning that – as their creator intended – do not have to be deciphered in minute detail: "If life is a game of cards, we are born without knowing the Rules. Yet we must play our hand. Is the Tarot only a card game, or is there a philosophy behind it?" •

Ibid; cover

Outside the circular portal to Mario Botta's fortress-like entrance building there is scarcely any suggestion of the secrets, of the fireworks in colours and shapes that are waiting for visitors a little further up the slope. There you suddenly find yourself in a kind of arena, the central place in the garden, dominated by the Magician, the High Priestess and the Empress, accompanied by six other figures. The Magician's mirrored tower salutes the distant landscape with raised hand. Below this, water pours out of the wide-open mouth of the blue High Priestess – a tribute to the Mouth of Hell in Bomarzo – over a broad cascade into a pool

The White Woman confronts the green dragon fearlessly and proves her strength.

The Magician salutes the distant landscape with a raised hand, while below him the High Priestess provides water and sets the stage for Jean Tinguely's Wheel of Fortune.

through which the Fool, a gaunt Skinny sculpture is wading. The Wheel of Fortune, one of Jean Tinguely's typical kinetic steel sculptures, provides the scene with additional movement. Tinguely, whom Niki met as early as the late fifties, introduced her to the Nouveau Réalistes circle. He was also – until his death in 1991 – the person with whom she shared her life and the congenial fellow artist without whose influence, co-operation and artistic interventions the Tarot Garden could not have become such an impressive Gesamtkunstwerk. Tinguely's rusty steel sculptures place important and finely balanced accents at all points where the lush quality of the ceramic, glass and mirrored sculptures almost threatens to get out of hand.

The great structure for the Empress, who symbolizes the archetype of the mother, is placed at the fringe of the central arena, sphinx-like, and adorned with a red crown. Niki de Saint-Phalle made this her studio and her home in 1980. The inside of this great sculpture is covered with mirror-glass mosaic and lit from circular windows in the tips of the voluptuous female figure's breasts. In those days, this was not just where she cooked, ate, slept and lived, it was also where she developed, together with Jean Tinguely, numerous artist friends and creative craftsmen, plans for the large reinforced concrete sculptures. Unlike the Skinnnies, which are filigree, transparent creations, these opulently shaped large-scale sculptures are reminiscent of the famous Nanas, and most of them can be entered or walked on. From the roof terrace with shower on the back of the Empress you enjoy one of the finest views of the Mediterranean landscape, though this has not remained unchanged in ensuing decades.

The Tarot Garden turned out much larger than expected, and swallowed more financial resources than originally intended. So in the early eighties, Niki de Saint Phalle decided to create her own range of per-

The Empress sits enthroned in Niki de Saint-Phalle's Tarot Garden like a colourful sphinx, providing the artist with a home for a long time.

This tower structure, symbolizing the patriarchy, is also part of the Emperor, the complex card of male power.

At the centre of the Emperor – the fourth Tarot card – is a courtyard with 22 differently designed columns surrounding two olive trees.

Access to the Emperor's enchanted castle courtyard is through a magical gate.

fumes, and invested the profits in extending her beloved garden. The sculpture of the Emperor shows how lavishly the work was pursued: he is in the form of a castle, with a magnificent, circular inner courtyard, a castle wall you can walk on and large defensive towers. In the inner courtyard, which is shaded by two trees, the relationship to Parc Güell is particularly clear: the 22 individually designed sculpted columns and the battlemented parapet with its curved concluding wall are formally very similar to Gaudí's masterpiece, but are considerably more expressive in their colour and surface design. This is closely connected with Niki de Saint-Phalle's biography: in the arcade – but by no means just here – she captured crucial elements of her tempestuous life for posterity, a life she was able to handle only through art. And this led to a work of art that was her life, the Tarot Garden, a sculpture garden as an individual interpretation of the world.

One of Tinguely's machines from hell pours out of the breaking tip of the mirror-glassed tower, symbolizing punishment by divine lightning.

The red rocket is also part of the male power figure that has the Emperor at its centre.

The moon can lend great imaginative force, but also awaken dark and dangerous powers, just like the power station that can be seen from the Tarot Garden.

The High Priest stands for faith, subjectivity and the search for personal happiness and redemption.

Niki de Saint-Phalle threw the mirrored outer skin of her sculpture round an existing olive tree like a glittering coat.

Rebellion against Modernism

"Let this be a new town, symbolic of the freedom of India, unfettered by the traditions of the past, an expression of the nation's faith in the future." This was the vision of Jawaharlal Nehru, the first prime minister of independent India, for the new provincial capital of Punjab. Chandigarh, one of the few realized planned cities of the 20th century, really did develop, under the direction of Le Corbusier, into an impressive urban monument for modern India. In the functionally structured street grid with icons of modern reinforced concrete architecture and lavish green spaces, it is only with difficulty that the essence of traditional Indian life makes its presence felt. And yet it does exist in a highly concentrated form in the mysterious Rock Garden on the north-western edge of the administrative town.

At the same time as Le Corbusier's grandiose visions were becoming built reality, Nek Chand, a humble street inspector in the Chandigarh Public Works Department started to realize his dream of a fairy-tale kingdom among the wild scrubland on the outskirts. In the planned city, where every building measure required planning permission, in contrast with other Indian cities, it was impossible even to clear undergrowth or build a little hut without official sanction. So Nek Chand worked secretly, often at night. From 1958 onwards he collected stones, rubble and material created by the demolition of old estates and the construction of the new town, and carted everything to his building site on a bicycle.

Design:
Nek Chand
Public park
Size: approx.
10 hectares
Under development
since 1965

The entrance to the rock garden leads through a solid concrete wall made up of barrel-shaped elements, crowned by white swans.

After collecting for seven years, this head-strong outsider started to create imaginative cement sculptures that he then artfully enhanced with scraps of coloured fabric, ceramic shards, glass splinters and other materials from his stocks. The collection of sculptures and stones eventually needed so much room that Nek Chand had to cultivate more and more space in order to make the wilderness into a worthy home for his creations at the end of the working day.

When the authorities wanted to clear the bush as part of their planned building measures in 1972, they were suddenly confronted with a colourful nation of about 2,000 sculptures. Confrontation with this illegally created world was a source of great indignation to the authorities. But in a short time all Chandigarh knew about Ned Chand's wonderful garden, and with the support of local contractors, who provided him with transport and materials, he was able to construct a series of smaller exhibition courtyards and thus conclude the first phase of the project successfully.

A few years later the authorities yielded to public pressure and opened the Rock Garden in 1976 as a municipal facility for whose upkeep and development Nek Chand was now officially responsible. Equipped with

Only a few steps into the garden it is quite clear that this is no ordinary garden, as all the walls are made of recycled materials and terra-cotta vessels.

A new little world awaits visitors at every twist in the pathway.

Narrow pathways accompany the river to the waterfall.

A group of Indian women and children, gracefully carrying water-jugs, as figures in the waterfall.

his own budget, a workforce of 50, building machinery, electricity and running water, the new Sub-Divisional Engineer, Rock Garden embarked with unrestrained creative vigour on the second development phase for his garden. Ultimately he felt called by God to make a gift to mankind and set a monument to tolerance and peace. New, larger exhibition courtyards were constructed, buildings and countless sculptures of people and animals came into being, a labyrinthine system of paths and water-courses developed, and last but not least he had to organize his material procurement better: an elaborate recycling programme guaranteed efficient collection and use of everything that could have been of use in any way, from bicycle saddles to fluorescent lighting tubes.

Unlike the building plans for the modern ideal city, the complex plan for the Rock Garden existed only in Nek Chand's head. Anyone entering his empire for the first time through the little entrance portal in the high garden wall topped with geese cannot have the slightest idea of what is waiting for him or her at the next bend in the narrow sunken path, over there behind the garden gate or in the next court-yard. A whole troop of monkeys might be looking curiously down, figures of girls carry their water-jugs to the well in an endless procession, or hundreds of decorative figures perform their ritual dance for one of the countless Indian deities who are undergoing one of their numerous incarnations in the figures. The imaginative world of the Rock Garden is as boundless as the ancient Indian sagas of gods and heroes like the Mahabharata and the Ramayana.

The garden, which can reasonably be called a park after the third development phase from 1983 on, now occupies about ten hectares. A large clearing in this park is reached via a deep, artificial gorge, past a rushing waterfall, in the shade of the trees and numerous palace-like

A city in the city of Chandigarh: the Rock Garden's temples sit proudly above the artificial gorge.

A world of their own for thousands of figures made of builders' rubble.

buildings on the hill. With its colourful ceramics and rustically cement-
ed arches the setting will almost remind Europeans a little of the Parc
Güell in Barcelona. A swing hangs in each of the 50 high arches, a feature much loved by children, while temples, amphitheatres and grot-
toes entice visitors to explore new terrain. The scene is populated with
numerous metre-high sculptures, and a high, illuminated tower will
soon be a sign for Nek Chand's paradise that can be seen from some
distance away.

Like all paradises, this one too is under threat, despite its international fame. It is only courageous resistance by residents that has prevent-
ed this imaginative alternative world to the ideal modern city from
having to give way to a road development project.

Graceful female figures with their
water-jugs.

An Indian Parc Güell? Nek Chand's
"big garden with swings."

Countless figures crouch like a troup
of monkeys on a carpet of white
ceramic fragments.

Terra-cotta dancers set off against a
white ceramic wall, four of a total of over
2,000 sculptures in the Rock Garden.

Thanks

The starting-point and basis for this book were 30 short garden portraits published between January 1999 and December 2003 in the regular "Gardens" column in the Neue Zürcher Zeitung's monthly NZZ FOLIO magazine. This series particularly helped interested amateurs to form an impression of current creative work in gardens and contemporary European landscape architecture. I would like to thank the Zurich landscape architect Andreas Tremp for prompting me to write for this prestigious Zurich magazine. I would also like to thank Lilli Binzegger and Daniel Weber, the managing editors of the NZZ FOLIO, personally for years of successful work together in a very pleasant and constructive atmosphere. I also have you two to thank among others for agreeing so readily that our joint commitment to disseminating new landscape architecture and garden art should appear in book form. My sincerest thanks for that as well.

Many garden owners and landscape architects readily allowed my wife Rita Weilacher and me into their garden paradises on our garden journeys around Europe. They also offered us illuminating background information and explained the concepts behind many interesting projects in detail. I should therefore like to thank them expressly once more for their commitment here as well.

I have now worked for over ten years on many successful Birkhäuser books with the Berlin-based editor Andreas Müller. Once more he has done all honour to his reputation as a conscientious, open-minded and committed editor. It was again a special pleasure to work on a new book project with him and his team, and also the Berlin graphic designer Bernd Fischer and the London translator Michael Robinson.

Without enthusiasm for new landscape architecture and garden art the quality of our environment would decline and books like this would not be written. I have been fortunate enough to share the delight I take in gardens for many years now with my wife: Rita! Many loving thanks! ... and certainly not just for reading my texts critically and constructively and for your careful photographic eye, for your patience and your tireless spirit of enterprise.